Publisher of C-Level Business Intelligence
www.Aspatore.com

Aspatore Books is the largest and most exclusive publisher of C-Level executives (CEO, CFO, CTO, CMO, Partner) from the world's most respected companies and law firms. Aspatore annually publishes a select group of C-Level executives from the Global 1,000, top 250 law firms (Partners & Chairs), and other leading companies of all sizes. C-Level Business Intelligence™, as conceptualized and developed by Aspatore Books, provides professionals of all levels with proven business intelligence from industry insiders – direct and unfiltered insight from those who know it best – as opposed to third-party accounts offered by unknown authors and analysts. Aspatore Books is committed to publishing an innovative line of business and legal books, those which lay forth principles and offer insights that when employed, can have a direct financial impact on the reader's business objectives, whatever they may be. In essence, Aspatore publishes critical tools – need-to-read as opposed to nice-to-read books – for all business professionals.

D0063032

DEAL TERMS

The Finer Points of Venture Capital Deal Structures,
Valuations, Term Sheets, Stock Options and
Getting Deals Done

Alex Wilmerding

Mat #40685999

BOOK & ARTICLE IDEA SUBMISSIONS

If you are a C-Level executive, senior lawyer, or venture capitalist interested in submitting a book or article idea to the Aspatore editorial board for review, please email AspatoreAuthors@thomson.com. Aspatore is especially looking for highly specific ideas that would have a direct financial impact on behalf of a reader. Completed publications can range from 2 to 2,000 pages. Include your book/article idea, biography, and any additional pertinent information.

©2005 Thomson/Aspatore
All rights reserved. Printed in the United States of America.

No part of this publication may be reproduced or distributed in any form or by any means, or stored in a database or retrieval system, except as permitted under Sections 107 or 108 of the U.S. Copyright Act, without prior written permission of the publisher. This book is printed on acid free paper.

Material in this book is for educational purposes only. This book is sold with the understanding that neither any of the authors or the publisher is engaged in rendering legal, accounting, investment, or any other professional service. Neither the publisher nor the authors assume any liability for any errors or omissions or for how this book or its contents are used or interpreted or for any consequences resulting directly or indirectly from the use of this book. For legal advice or any other, please consult your personal lawyer or the appropriate professional.

The views expressed by the individuals in this book (or the individuals on the cover) do not necessarily reflect the views shared by the companies they are employed by (or the companies mentioned in this book). The employment status and affiliations of authors with the companies referenced are subject to change.

Aspatore books may be purchased for educational, business, or sales promotional use. For information, please email AspatoreStore@thomson.com.

A special thanks to all the individuals that made this book possible.

Special thanks to: Kirsten Catanzano, Melissa Conradi, Molly Logan, Justin Hallberg

ISBN 1-58762-208-4

For corrections, updates, comments or any other inquiries please email AspatoreEditorial@thomson.com.

First Printing, 2003
10 9 8 7 6 5 4 3 2 1

DEAL TERMS

Table of Contents

FOREWORD

The venture capital arena is complex, dynamic, and equally challenging for entrepreneurs and members of the financial community. *Deal Terms* has been written with the goal to provide entrepreneurs and members of the financial community with a set of tools and perspectives that will help them better navigate the complexities of early- and expansion-stage venture capital financings. While my first book, *Term Sheets and Valuations,* provides an analysis from both company and investor perspectives of each of the terms in a typical term sheet, *Deal Terms* drills down to provide in-depth analysis of the core issues that are addressed in private equity and debt financing term sheets and the context surrounding these financings.

The term sheet provides a snapshot of and roadmap to a financing and the issues that entrepreneurs and financial professionals commit to capturing in closing documents for a financing. However, not only can it be argued that no single term in a term sheet is more or less important than any other, but also it is unlikely that any two lawyers could ever agree on a true "neutral" form of a term sheet – or so asserts Jim Crane, a private equity lawyer in Boston who contributes to a dialogue on this subject in Chapter Eight. As a refresher or point of reference, a so-called "neutral" form of a term sheet is included in the appendices.

It is in this context that *Deal Terms* drills down on the core subjects that concern entrepreneurs and private equity financial professionals alike and that are central to term sheets and the financings they typically give rise to. The first five chapters of the book focus on valuations, the relationship between common and preferred stock, dilution, options, flat rounds, and down rounds. These chapters are, on balance, quite technical; more qualitative information is featured in Chapters Six through Nine.

Chapter One examines company valuations and features two case studies that analyze the ways in which investors establish valuations and the effects of multiple rounds of financing on valuation, investor returns, and a company's capital structure. For a refresher on the time value of money, consult the tables featured in the appendix. These will at least illuminate the predictable effects of compounding interest, which have implications in so many aspects of private equity financings and in our own financial lives.

The second chapter of the book analyzes the extent to which different types of preferred stock affect how the interests of preferred and common stockholders can be aligned and are intertwined. Chapter Three focuses on dilution, a sensitive issue for both founders and investors. It considers the mechanics of dilution and the contrasting effects that different dilution formulas can have on the value of securities when exercised. The subject of stock options and their effect on capital structures is examined in Chapter Four; a detailed study on the treatment of advisors and board members is included and also featured in this book's appendices. Chapter Five discusses the implications of flat rounds and down rounds, often reflected in term sheets during soft markets when prior valuations for a company may have been too high or after a period in which a company has failed to perform to plan.

The last four chapters of the book consider the implications of alternatives to private equity financing and provide perspective on the context surrounding them and the road that companies are likely to follow from term sheet to closing. Chapter Six analyzes the implications of debt and bridge financing and features an example of a term sheet used in financing convertible promissory notes, sometimes referred to as "bridge financing."

Chapter Seven provides perspective on the business assessment and due diligence that is likely to be conducted by investors before and after the term sheet phase and illustrates the extent to which entrepreneurs need to be well prepared for this process, which involves far more than just assembling relevant legal and financial documents into binders. This qualitative assessment is complemented by a list of documents likely to be requested during due diligence; the list is included in this book's appendix. Chapter Eight assesses the "dos and don'ts" of successful financings from the perspectives of experienced private equity counsel. These perspectives provide advice on what to look out for in a term sheet, how to navigate the complex landscape before a closing, and how to coordinate venture firms, legal teams, and company management. Finally, Chapter Nine offers advice and anecdotes for raising capital from the perspective of experienced and seasoned entrepreneurs. The first of two perspectives explores the experience of Andrew McKee, who successfully founded and exited Vacation.com and now works as general partner to a venture firm. His discussion highlights the trade-offs that exist between financing in different forms – debt and private equity – and from different sources – angels and strategic and financial investors. The chapter concludes with a discussion of the merits of placement agents in the fundraising process from the perspective of Ginny Davis Wilmerding, who managed private placement relationships as part of the fundraising process for two start-ups.

Acknowledgements

The material that has been incorporated into this book reflects directly and indirectly the perspectives of many colleagues from portfolio companies and venture firms throughout the private equity landscape. I am particularly grateful for the contributions and advice provided by Graham Anderson of EuclidSR Partners; Tom Claflin of Claflin Capital Management; Jim Crane, most recently of Testa, Hurwitz & Thibeault; Jeff Donohue of Kirkpatrick & Lockhart; Sarah Reed of Charles River Ventures; and not least of all my wife, Virginia Davis Wilmerding, currently with the Harvard Business School.

Doubtless, the content of this book also reflects the experience and perspective I have gleaned from assignments in industry, as well as from serving as a principal at Boston Capital Ventures and on numerous company and not-for-profit boards. It is indeed a privilege to work in the private equity industry with so many impressive entrepreneurs and members of the financial and legal community. This book is intended to serve as a resource to provide greater transparency into the world of venture capital.

1

COMPANY VALUATION

In This Chapter . . .

Every entrepreneur who aspires to raise capital looks forward to "talking valuation" with potential investors. Some dream about it, only to wonder, once a deal has closed, what exactly they have agreed to. Whereas the central chapter of my previous book, *Term Sheets and Valuations*, serves to demystify many seemingly complex terms of a financing by explaining their implications, the topic of valuation and how it is determined warrants a chapter of its own.

Many people end a negotiation, agree to terms, and walk away unclear as to how the final valuation of the company was determined. The entire topic of valuation is often shrouded in mystery, largely because of the private nature of the venture capital industry and the extent to which valuation methodology is rarely openly discussed. A valuation is a function of a myriad of elements, none of which will necessarily apply equally when assessing any two companies. Factors that influence a valuation include:

o   The current and expected future valuations of comparable companies in the public and, when available, private marketplace
o   The supply and demand for capital at the time of financing
o   Intangibles unique to a specific company, including the quality of a management team, a company's competitive advantage, and its likely pace of revenue growth and profitability
o   The nature and timing of an expected exit for the investor
o   The implications of future capital raises, as well as needs to expand a company's options pool on the company's capital structure, going forward

Confidentiality

In this chapter, we will examine some of the methodologies applied by venture capitalists in determining valuation. Before doing so, it is important to understand why discussion of valuation is most often a private or confidential matter for most private companies.

Entrepreneurs and VCs alike benefit from keeping the financial structures, terms, and valuations of each company confidential until a company does a road show before an IPO or is brought to the table to discuss a sale by a prospective acquirer. Even when a company is on a fast track to a future round of financing or on the block to be acquired, documenting valuation in the press or in trade circles establishes a data point that can be used to decipher a company's revenues, assess the value investors are placing on the company's technology or offering, and even bias how a subsequent round of financing may be approached by outside investors or by a future acquirer. Doing so may also negatively bias existing and prospective customers. Companies often announce the closing of a financing and report the amount raised; when substantial, this signals staying power to existing and potential customers, as well as the competition. Reporting a post-money valuation in essence allows a competitor or potential acquirer to decipher more information about a company than may be strategically advantageous in the future.

When a company does announce a valuation, it may do so to send a clear message, perhaps to a potentially crowded space or to potential acquirers. This can be a way to signal to the market and to customers that a company has a sustainable business, is gaining momentum and credibility, and is well ahead of existing or prospective new entrants. A private company that is in the process of expanding and has yet to become cash-flow positive may feel that in announcing an impressive valuation and round of financing through a press release, it can signal market leadership in a potentially crowded space. Assuming that such a round has been led by a new investor and included the participation of existing investors, the market will likely interpret such an announcement as validation that an existing player has produced significant shareholder value.

Perhaps prospective investors of earlier-stage competitors will take heed. But such tactics have clear downside. If the same company fails to execute to plan and goes back to the market 12 months later for financing, competitors and outside investors could suspect damaged goods. In an uncrowded market vertical, crowing about the high valuations investors have provided a company can be the rallying cry that motivates other investors and VCs to consider backing new entrants.

Fair Market Value and the Use of Comparables

There are two generally accepted ways to determine fair market value for a company. The first assesses cash flows on a going forward basis to determine a present value. The second approach determines value by looking at comparable companies to come up with a fair valuation. Both require close examination and assessment of the nature, quality, and predictability of future revenue streams, as well as earnings before interest, depreciation, and taxes (EBITDA).

Using cash flows to determine value is generally not the primary and sole methodology applied by VCs in determining valuation; this is especially true in early-stage companies, which are by nature not yet cash flow positive. For later-stage investors who invest only in profitable companies, doing so can make great sense. My assumption in providing guidance on valuation methodology in this book is that most readers are interested in how valuations are determined for unprofitable, start-up, early-stage, or expansion-stage companies. For a good explanation of the use of cash flows to determine value, I recommend a core finance text used by Columbia Business School, *Analysis for Financial Management,* by Robert C. Higgins.

To briefly summarize Higgins, by assessing cash flows one can generate a present value for a company by adding together the net present value of cash flows for the first five to six years of growth in a company with the net present value of a terminal value assigned the company. The terminal value captures the cash flows for the future life of the company subsequent to the first five- to six-year period and is determined by placing a value based on assumptions about future growth and cost of capital on the subsequent period of cash flows.

Comparables are the cornerstone of valuation analysis for most VCs. VCs typically use comparables to determine a likely future exit value for an investment. Higgins may also be useful for a more detailed discussion of comparables in valuation analysis. He states:

> Use of comparables in business valuation requires equal parts of art and science. First it is necessary to decide which ...companies are most similar to the target and then determine what the share prices of the publicly traded companies imply for the FMV (fair market value) of the firm in question....We begin our search for comparables by considering firms in the same, or closely

related, industries with similar growth prospects and capital structures. *(p. 343)*

A venture investor is therefore likely first to determine which basket of mature or liquid existing companies in the investor's opinion most closely resembles the profile to which a contemplated investment aspires. It is important to note that an investor's choice of comparables may work at cross purposes with the goals of the entrepreneur. One basket of comparables may point to a future valuation that is lower than that which an alternative basket of comparables could otherwise support. Whereas there may well be arguments for choosing one basket of comparables over another, investors have specific goals beyond using comparables to determine whether a specific rate of return can be generated. Investors often also want to own a specific percentage of a total company or of a specific round of financing to be assured of a specific degree of influence, should a shareholder vote be required. The choice of comparables and the discount rate therefore have a direct influence on the ultimate ownership percentage an investment will buy.

While the balance sheet of a start-up, early-stage, or expansion-stage company is unlikely to resemble that of a mature or public company at a time of VC financing, the aspiring company's business plan should be compelling enough to point to the company achieving a profile comparable to that of more mature companies in a matter of years. Assuming, therefore, that the prospective investment meets its objectives, it is possible to interpolate, based on market data at the time of a proposed private equity financing, both an appropriate current market-based valuation and an appropriate and likely value at some future contemplated time of exit. The most common ratios used to compare one business to another include market value of the firm value/revenue, firm/EBIT (Earnings Before Interest and Taxes), and market value of the firm/EBITDA (Earnings Before Interest, Taxes and Depreciation).

A critical factor in determining a company's future value as a private company or likely acquisition candidate, rather than as a stand-alone public entity, is the "Public Company Premium" or "Private Market Discount." Data tracking these ratios for private equity transactions and middle market M&A transactions are published in *The Daily Deal. Portfolio Management Data* also publishes M&A statistics.

Because venture investments are typically held for several years, determining the value of an investment requires ascertaining whether a current price reflects sufficient growth to allow the investor to generate a return that meets the investor's cost of capital. Alternatively, the investor can work to determine the likely value of a company at some future point and discount that value to the present. Because the future value assigned a company will vary significantly depending on whether a company is sold or goes public, the future value assigned a company must also reflect whichever assumption is preferred by the investor. In either case, the discount rate used to discount future values to the present has a significant effect on the present value attributed to an investment. For venture investors, the discount rate applied will vary. As discussed earlier, it would not be atypical for an early-stage venture investor to expect and to assume a discount rate that reflects a rate of return of 50 percent. Later-stage investors will be more likely to assume discount rates of 35 percent to 40 percent. The appendix tables in this book highlight the magnitude of the effect of a discount rate on the time value of money and should be consulted.

The extent to which valuation is an art becomes clear as we consider the variability of factors that are critical to assessing a company's likely future worth. A valuation must work closely to project how the market will view an asset at a specific future period of time, how sustainable the growth rate of a company is, and how predictably a group of companies with which the prospective investment is likely to be compared are likely to grow and be supported by the marketplace. Economic cycles and the capacity of a specific sector will necessarily influence these ratios. The venture investor who over- or under-estimates the strength of ratios and growth rates on a going-forward basis will therefore fail to come close to accurately valuing a company.

The market may, for example, assign revenue multiples of seven times revenues to a basket of companies growing at 50 percent today, but in three years assign multiples of only four because the market as a whole has come off, growth rates for the company and the basket of companies to which the company is best compared have dropped, and a sector is filled with overcapacity. A company could therefore hit its revenue target of $100 million in three years but find that to be acquired, the market will pay only $400 million, as compared to the $700 million price tag the venture capitalist assumed in a valuation analysis.

It is precisely because VCs recognize that clairvoyance is not one of their strengths and that accurately predicting markets, time to liquidity, and management performance is an art form that they work so hard to engineer financial structures and term sheets to provide significant protections. Liquidation preference is one such tool. Building in an accruing dividend and an interest rate attached to a preferred class of security also adds to the value of the preferred. If a VC can get guaranteed liquidation preference for investors of up to four times the value of the preferred in a well financed deal, investors can likely lock in a return of 41 percent or better, as long as the investment creates enough value to be purchased or go public within four years, the management team has adequate incentive under such a scenario, and sufficient powers exist to enforce this right.

Case Study:
Comparables Analysis in Determining Valuation

In 1999, Case.com, a company that had an Internet-based service offering, planned to raise $15 million from the private equity market. The company aspired to have $10 million in revenues 12 months from the time of financing. Its revenues at the time of financing were virtually non-existent – $500,000 for the prior 12 months. The company looked for a pre-money valuation of between $20 million and $30 million and secured one at $30 million. How did the investors and the marketplace justify this?

The selection of comparables used by investors was a critical component in determining the value of the company at that time. If one agreed that Case.com was comparable to public Internet advertising and content companies at the time, and the basket of comparables included such companies as America Online, DoubleClick, Excite, Infoseek, and Yahoo!, the median ratio of market value divided by revenues for the preceding calendar year (1998) for this basket as a whole was roughly 11 times. Looking forward at the time to projected year-end 1999 revenues – 12 months out – this ratio dropped to about eight times.

Because of the unique nature of the business of the company seeking financing, it was equally possible to consider as a basket of comparables a selection of enabling technology and Internet software companies, including names such as Exodus, Netscape, and VeriSign. Such companies had on average generated market caps of more than 22 times revenues in 1998 and were expected to generate market caps of more than ten times revenues by year-end 1999.

When applying these ratios to the projections of Case.com and looking only at year-end 1999 revenues, it was therefore logical to argue that on a forward revenues basis the hypothetical value of the company would, were it treated like a public company and compared to these two baskets of companies, be eight to ten times 1999 revenues. This would imply a firm value of $80 million to $100 million for a company with projected revenues of just $10 million on a going forward basis. Clearly, however, this valuation methodology would be considered inappropriate because the company seeking financing was private. So a "Private Market Discount" of 50 percent was applied to the company. As a result of this discount, it was possible to justify the value of the company post-money as between $40 million and $50 million. Case.com could therefore raise $15 million at a pre-money valuation of $30 million and make investors comfortable with a post-money valuation of $45 million, a number right in the middle of the range.

Why was such an analysis sufficient to make investors comfortable? How did this valuation satisfy the investor's need for a 50 percent-plus annualized return? The company's growth rate provides us with the answer.

Had the projected annualized growth for Case.com been in the range of 10 percent, based on the valuation given the company, it would be difficult to see how an investor with an expectation of

50 percent annualized returns could ever generate a satisfactory exit. The investor would need extraordinary terms and have to expect to change the course of the company and beat the market to comfortably expect an annualized return of 50 percent or greater. If the investor assumed $10 million in revenues 12 months from financing, and a simple 10 percent revenue growth rate over the subsequent four years, it is likely that the company's revenues would stand at only $14.6 million at the end of year five. Assuming that the market multiples of eight to ten times revenues remain the same in five years, the market valuation of the company in five years would range from $116.8 million to $146 million on the public market, or just $58.4 million to $73 million on the private market.

In our example, $15 million from new investors purchased 33 percent of the company. If we assume that in five years, the company raises $25 million on the public market at a post-money valuation of $145 million, the pre-money valuation would be $120 million, of which the new investors' value would, assuming a straight convertible with no guaranteed returns, represent 33 percent, or $40 million. This would represent an annualized return of slightly over 20 percent – well below the investors' assumed cost of capital. In fact, the investor would need to receive all of the pre-money value of $120 million to generate slightly more than a 50 percent return over five years. There is very little chance the company would agree to terms that would allow this and therefore little likelihood that at such pricing and with a mere 10 percent in annualized growth, the deal would take place.

In our example, however, Case.com's expected revenue growth rate per annum was 50 percent. Equally important, the annualized projected growth of earnings for the five-year period for the company was comparable to that for the two baskets of comparable public companies.

Effects of the Financing Environment and Intangibles

The supply of and demand for capital play an important but measured role in the valuation a company is likely to command. Capital is most restricted or expensive and valuations under greatest pressure during and following a period involving a sudden market correction or a downturn in the economy. None of us has a crystal ball for future economic growth; pricing is therefore more a function of the current or most recent nature of the marketplace.

During periods of economic softening or market correction, the public markets, as well as the market for mergers and acquisitions, are in flux and directly affect venture investors' valuation analyses. Venture investors look to the prices established in the marketplace to put a prospective exit value on their investments. The values investors are willing to pay in a public offering and the values corporations are willing to pay to make acquisitions come under pressure and typically decline during a market correction or economic downturn. There is consequential downward pressure on valuations during these periods and, at times, a disconnect between a company's expectations with respect to valuation and those of investors. As a result, the feeling in the marketplace is a tightening of sources of capital.

A number of intangible elements influence the ultimate valuation an investor is willing to give a company. These intangible elements are all factored into an investors' assessment of risk.

First and most important, assessment of management quality and experience will directly influence assumptions regarding how an investor's ownership percentage may change over time. The more management needs to be augmented, the greater the potential dilution that future needs in terms of options will have on the ultimate ownership percentage of an investor. Most investors generally start with the assumption that a base of at least 10 percent of the capitalization of the company needs to be provided for management. This figure can grow to up to 20 percent, depending on holes in the management team.

Second, assumptions about revenue growth are often a source of disagreement between entrepreneurs and investors. They are arguably somewhat fungible, particularly when signed contracts cannot be used to support an entreprencur's projections.

Third, every company has unique product development, as well as customer adoption risk. How an investor assumes either will pan out for a company will influence the investor's assumptions regarding revenue growth.

Fourth, the strength of a company's competitive advantage and ability to create escalating barriers to entry are sometimes debatable.

Fifth, the quality of the business plan and the market data, as well as testimonials, is important not only for a current round, but also in positioning a company for subsequent rounds of financing.

Finally, and perhaps most intangible, the "sexiness" of a deal in the eyes of an investor can work for and against a company. Beauty is truly in the eye of the beholder. A space perceived to be hot and inflated will typically come under valuation pressure. While the best venture investors are drawn to investments in industries they know well, it is difficult to predict how their industry bias and personal experience will influence their valuation.

Risk and Exit Strategy for Investors

Intangible risk is a very subjective measure when it comes to evaluating and valuing an investment. Similarly, the extent to which a company and an investor agree on likely future revenue and earnings and the timing and nature of an exit reflect the assessment of both parties of future risk.

Investors will typically adjust future revenue and earnings projections to reflect the investor's individual assessment of risk related to an investment. In the same vein, the VC is likely to adjust assumptions with regard to exit valuations and length of holding of an investment to factor in conservative assumptions about the likely timing, value, and nature of a prospective exit.

The company that assumes with dead certainty it can go public at a specific valuation in a specific number of years is likely to be gravely disappointed by the valuation given by an investor who assumes that company is likely to generate an exit in a longer period of time through a private sale that might well be priced at a discount to the public markets.

Future Capital Needs

The extent to which companies will or may require future rounds of financing creates the opportunity for further disparity between the valuations placed on a company by investors and by its founders and employees. VCs will almost always assume that earlier-stage companies will require more time and more financing than the company projects. Management teams who believe they can do more with less, in less time, are the source of the entrepreneurial drive that ultimately propels a company forward. But more often companies face unforeseen challenges that require additional funding or slow the pace of progress.

The time value of money is a critical and central factor in how investors establish their projections. When investors feel it is prudent to allocate more time and more money in their assessment of the investment horizon for a company, valuations are inevitably affected and drawn down.

Case Study:
Relationship of Dilution,
Valuation, and Investor Return

To truly appreciate the relationship between dilution, valuation, and investor return, consider the case of Dilution.com, a study that has been prepared with the help of Graham Anderson, General Partner at EuclidSR Partners in New York.

Dilution.com approached a venture firm in the hope of raising $4,000,000 to fund a Series B Preferred round. Management owned 4,500,000 shares, or 90 percent, of Dilution.com and had sold 10 percent, or 500,000 shares, to the Preferred A investors in the prior financing at $1 per share. The value of the company was $5,000,000 post-money after the prior round. See the cap table entitled *Dilution.Com Preferred A Financing,* below, for a snapshot of the capital structure before the Series B financing.

Dilution.com Preferred A Financing

	COMMON	COST	PFD A $1.00	COST	PFD B $1.00	COST	PFD C $1.00	COST	WARRANTS	OPTIONS	TOTAL SHARES	% OWNED	TOTAL COST	SHARE VALUE	TOTAL CASH IN	% CASH IN
INVESTORS																
Pfd A			500,000	$500,000							500,000	10.0%	$500,000	$500,000	$500,000	100.0%
Pfd B											0	0.0%	$0	$0	$0	0.0%
Pfd C											0	0.0%	$0	$0	$0	0.0%
MANAGEMENT																
Managers	4,500,000	$0									4,500,000	90.0%	$0	$4,500,000	$0	0.0%
Options											0	0.0%	$0	$0	$0	0.0%
TOTALS	4,500,000	$0	500,000	$500,000	0	$0	0	$0	0	0	5,000,000	100.0%	$500,000	$5,000,000	$500,000	100.0%
PRE-ROUND 1	$4,500,000															
POST-ROUND 1	$5,000,000															

Venture Capital Percentage   10.0%

Management Percentage   90.0%

The venture firm agreed to invest $4,000,000 in the Preferred B financing at $1.15 per share. However, 2,000,000 options were created at this time because the venture firm and the company agreed that additional management needed to be hired. This raised the pre-money valuation of the company to $8,050,000. But the capital structure of the company was changed dramatically as an option pool of 2,000,000 options was created in addition to the 5,000,000 shares that existed after the Series A financing. When adding the value of the 3,478,261 new shares purchased by the venture investor at $1.15 per share, the post-money valuation of the company was then $12,050,000. Despite the option pool that had been created, management's ownership dropped from 90 percent of the company to 62 percent of the company, and the venture investor's ownership increased from 10 percent of the company after the Series A financing to 38 percent of the company after the Series B financing. See the cap table titled *Dilution.com Preferred B Financing,* below, to track the effects on the capital structure after the Preferred B financing.

Dilution.com Preferred B Financing

	COMMON	COST	PFD A $1.00	COST	PFD B $1.15	COST	PFD C $1.15	COST	WARRANTS	OPTIONS	TOTAL SHARES	% OWNED	TOTAL COST	SHARE VALUE	TOTAL CASH IN	% CASH IN
INVESTORS																
Pfd A			500,000	$500,000							500,000	4.8%	$500,000	$575,000	$500,000	11.1%
Pfd B					3,478,261	$4,000,000					3,478,261	33.2%	$4,000,000	$4,000,000	$4,000,000	88.9%
Pfd C											0	0.0%	$0	$0	$0	0.0%
MANAGEMENT																
Managers	4,500,000	$0									4,500,000	42.9%	$0	$5,175,000	$0	0.0%
Options										2,000,000	2,000,000	19.1%	$0	$2,300,000	$0	0.0%
TOTALS	4,500,000	$0	500,000	$500,000	3,478,261	$4,000,000	0	$0	0	2,000,000	10,478,261	100.0%	$4,500,000	$12,050,000	$4,500,000	100.0%
PRE-ROUND 2	$8,050,000												Venture Capital Percentage			38.0%
POST-ROUND 2	$12,050,000												Management Percentage			62.0%

The management team and Preferred A investors of Dilution.com were thrilled with the 15 percent improvement in share price that resulted in the pricing of the Series B round. They finally bit the bullet and accepted the pricing offered them because the Preferred B venture investor convinced them that, in its analysis, the company was likely to require an additional $15,000,000 in financing, an event that would be dilutive to everyone.

The good news was that Dilution.com went on to raise $15,000,000 in a Series C financing at $1.91 per share, roughly the pricing the Series B venture investor predicted the market would bear. It is important to note that while the value of the price per share in the company increased, the original $4,000,000 ownership percentage of the Series B investor dropped from 33 percent to 19 percent, in line with the same drop in ownership percentage experienced by management, whose ownership percentage dropped from 62 percent to 35.5 percent. Further good news was that after the Series C financing, the company went on to meet its milestones and was sold for $75,000,000, roughly what the Series B venture investor had predicted. Management received $26,625,000, or 35.5 percent of the proceeds, as a result of the transaction; the Series B received $14,250,000 for its 19 percent ownership interest. See the cap table titled *Dilution.com Preferred C Financing,* below, to consider the profile of the company after the Series C financing and at the time of the company's ultimate sale.

Dilution.com Preferred C Financing

	COMMON	PFD A $1.00	COST	PFD B $1.15	COST	PFD C $1.91	COST	WARRANTS	OPTIONS	TOTAL SHARES	% OWNED	TOTAL COST	SHARE VALUE	TOTAL CASH IN	% CASH IN
INVESTORS															
Pfd A		500,000	$500,000							500,000	2.7%	$500,000	$955,000	$500,000	2.6%
Pfd B				3,478,261	$4,000,000					3,478,261	19.0%	$4,000,000	$6,643,478	$4,000,000	20.5%
Pfd C						7,853,403	$15,000,000			7,853,403	42.8%	$15,000,000	$15,000,000	$15,000,000	76.9%
MANAGEMENT															
Managers	4,500,000		$0							4,500,000	24.5%	$0	$8,595,000	$0	0.0%
Options									2,000,000	2,000,000	10.9%	$0	$3,820,000	$0	0.0%
TOTALS	4,500,000	500,000	$500,000	3,478,261	$4,000,000	7,853,403	$15,000,000	0	2,000,000	18,331,664	100.0%	$19,500,000	$35,013,478	$19,500,000	100.0%
PRE-ROUND 3	$20,013,478											Venture Capital Percentage		64.5%	
POST ROUND 3	$35,013,478											Management Percentage		35.5%	

The Series B venture investor and management did well by the transaction. How well? The Series B investor initially had priced the Series B round hoping to achieve a return of slightly more than 50 percent over a two-year period. The Series B financing closed in May 1999. In their initial valuation analysis, the Series B venture investor focused on the revenue growth and the likely exit strategy for Dilution.com and, working back from these assumptions, assumed Dilution.com would sell for roughly $75,000,000 in two years. Had the company indeed been sold in May 2002 at this price, the Series B investor's return would have been about 54 percent. Because the company ultimately was sold months earlier, in October 2001, Series B investor's actual return was in excess of 72 percent. The investor received the same multiple of 3.6 times what it would have received in May 2002, but the timing of the investment exit had a direct effect on the percentage return on capital. See the IRR Calculation for Sale in May 2002 titled *Dilution.com IRR Analysis,* below, and compare this to the IRR Calculation for Sale in October 2001.

Dilution.com IRR Analysis

May 99	(4,000,000)	May 99	(4,000,000)
Jun 99	-	Jun 99	-
Jul 99	-	Jul 99	-
Aug 99	-	Aug 99	-
Sep 99	-	Sep 99	-
Oct 99	-	Oct 99	-
Nov 99	-	Nov 99	-
Dec 99	-	Dec 99	-
Jan 00	-	Jan 00	-
Feb 00	-	Feb 00	-
Mar 00	-	Mar 00	-
Apr 00	-	Apr 00	-
May 00	-	May 00	-
Jun 00	-	Jun 00	-
Jul 00	-	Jul 00	-
Aug 00	-	Aug 00	-
Sep 00	-	Sep 00	-
Oct 00	-	Oct 00	-
Nov 00	-	Nov 00	-
Dec 00	-	Dec 00	-
Jan 01	-	Jan 01	-
Feb 01	-	Feb 01	-
Mar 01	-	Mar 01	-
Apr 01	-	Apr 01	-
May 01	-	May 01	*
Jun 01	-	Jun 01	-
Jul 01	-	Jul 01	-
Aug 01	-	Aug 01	-
Sep 01	-	Sep 01	-
Oct 01	-	10/15/01 Fair Market Value	14,226,087
Nov 01	-		
Dec 01	-	Internal ROR	72.25%
Jan 02	-	Multiple of Invested Capital	3.6
Feb 02	-		

↑ Assumes Dilution.com sold for $75,000,000 in 10/01. Pfd. B shareholders own approx. 19% at sale.

Mar 02	-
Apr 02	-
5/15/02 Fair Market Value	14,226,087
Internal ROR	54.50%
Multiple of Invested Capital	3.6

←Assumes Dilution.com sold for $75,000,000 in 5/02. Pfd. B shareholders own approx. 19% at sale.

As in our earlier case study, the Series B investor had, at the time of the pricing for the Series B preferred, assumed a high correlation coefficient between revenue growth and price appreciation for public Internet companies. This high correlation between revenue growth and price also appeared to hold true for private M&A Internet transactions at the time. The Series B preferred investor was also acutely aware that later-stage investors were pricing deals based on historical revenue numbers and forward revenue numbers at the time of the Series B financing and assumed this would hold true two years out from the Series B financing. Factoring in the dilutive effect of a subsequent $15,000,000 financing at an assumed $1.91 per share, the Series B investor could predict its ownership percentage would be roughly 19 percent of the company at the time of sale.

Venture Investors Need To Shoot for High Returns

It is rare that at the timing of a financing an investor can accurately predict the exact pricing of subsequent financings and the exact value of an ultimate exit valuation. Only rarely might a strategic investor invest at one valuation on the stipulation that the investor be able to exercise within a fixed period of time an option to acquire at some pre-negotiated value the company in which it has invested.

In this second case study, you may assume that the Series B investor invested with remarkable clairvoyance to emphasize the effect the timing of an exit has on the percentage rate of return for the investor. As I pointed out earlier, no VC can reliably predict the future – the story has been simplified for illustration purposes. While this case study may help the entrepreneur understand the dilutive effects of additional options and subsequent financings on a company's capital structure, the case study also emphasizes the effect an investor's assumptions about the value of future financings and exits will have on pricing.

Both of the last two spreadsheets featured in the previous case highlight returns of between 50 percent and 70 percent-plus. In defense of venture investors, the probability of an entire portfolio achieving returns in this range is very low. The reason these returns represent a range within which investors often establish their own targets for annual returns is that the total basket of investments a venture firm may make is likely to include a range of returns. Whereas some companies may be completely written off, others will earn handsome returns, sometimes in excess of ten times invested capital. If a venture firm has, for example, established expectations among its investors that the firm will aim to generate, for example, a 25 percent to 30 percent annualized return for the total portfolio, it will need to generate a significantly higher return to compensate for the VC firm's operating costs, which generally may account for 2 percent of capital committed to a fund. This is to say that a fund that raises $50 million in commitments from investors and draws down 2 percent per year in operating costs over seven years will have only $43 million available for investment. Consider the following table:

m = million

	Yr. 1	Yr. 2	Yr. 3	Yr. 4	Yr. 5	Yr. 6	Yr. 7	Multiple
Co. A	-3 m		-2 m			6 m		1.20 x
Co. B	-4 m	-1 m			9 m			1.80 x
Co. C	-2 m	-1 m		8 m				2.65 x
Co. D.	-1 m	-2 m		4 m				1.33 x
Co. E	-4 m						5 m	1.25 x
Co. F	-5 m						6 m	1.20 x

Co. G	-2 m	-1 m	17 m					5.66 x
Co. H	-2 m	-2 m			-1 m	-1 m	43 m	7.16 x
Co. I	-3 m	-1 m	-1 m		17 m			3.40 x
Co. J	-1 m	-1 m	-1 m	-1 m			7 m	1.75 x
Fees	-1 m	-1 m	-1 m	-1 m	-1 m	-1 m	-1 m	
Cash flow (before profits)	-28 m	-10 m	12 m	10 m	24 m	4 m	60 m	110 m
Cash flow (after profits)	-28 m	-10 m	12 m	10 m	24 m	4 m	48 m	98 m

Several assumptions have been made to simplify this example. Investor capital is assumed to be contributed about the time it was invested or spent by the venture firm on fees, with the exception of year seven, when fees are drawn out of the cash flows generated by liquidated investments. The term of the limited partnership, the typical investment vehicle venture capital investors would use, is assumed to be seven years, and the fee schedule to be flat. But in the real world, limited partnerships may have lives of up to ten years and fee schedules that decline during the later life of the partnership.

Finally, all calculations with respect to returns are made after profits to the venture capital management team. Typically, venture firms earn 20 percent of profits. In this example, $50 million was committed by investors, and $110 million was generated in cash flow as net proceeds from investments. Ninety-eight million dollars is actually returned to investors because $12 million, or 20 percent of the $60 million in profits, is distributed to the venture firm.

This series of ten investments represents a 25 percent annualized return on capital for investors. The range of returns on invested capital by company is between 1.2 and 7.2 times. While venture firms will typically invest in new companies over a series of years, this example highlights how venture firms look at the projected returns of any one company in the context of the likely performance of an overall portfolio. The example highlights the extent to which the timing and multiples of return on any one investment affects the return for investors.

2

COMMON AND PREFERRED STOCK AND EFFECTS ON VALUATION

In This Chapter . . .

The capital structure that ultimately will be created upon consummation of a financing directly reflects the core terms stipulated and agreed to in a term sheet between a venture firm or syndicate of investors and a company. One of the core issues upon which entrepreneurs are wise to focus is the relationship between preferred and common stock as stipulated in the term sheet. This relationship can vary significantly and can, depending on the terms negotiated, produce significantly different capital structures and economic outcomes.

I have worked closely with a number of firms with the goal to assemble syndicates of investors capable of committing the amount of capital a growing company desires to reach cash flow break-even. While each firm often has its own hot buttons and preferred method of structuring a term sheet, syndicates always agree to the terms in a term sheet, fully cognizant of the capital structure that will be created or effected as a result of a pending financing and the specific relationship stipulated between preferred and common stockholders.

There are two traditional approaches to structuring venture capital investments and to creating a class of security with which outside investors, venture or angel, will be comfortable. The first uses straight common stock. The second uses convertible preferred stock to accommodate institutional or later-stage investors while maintaining common stock for founders and early-stage angel investors. Both approaches have merits.

The Relationship Between Common and Preferred Stock

Often misunderstood by the entrepreneur are the nuances in the ways convertible preferred stock and common stock function as part of the capital structure. Use of convertible preferred stock to accommodate venture or outside investors clearly distinguishes the preferred from the common; the interests of both types of security are most clearly and technically aligned when conversion of the preferred into common actually comes about. But this usually happens only at an IPO or sale of the company; in the meantime, preferred stockholders have many rights and preferences that the common stockholders do not have.

The relationship between the two classes of stock is largely a function of the relationship between a company's pace of growth and the Liquidation Preference and Redemption features the convertible preferred requires. When an investor purchases only convertible preferred, the relationship between the preferred and the common is pretty straightforward; preferred investors are entirely ahead of common in the company's capital structure. A number of firms use a third approach that results in the sale of both straight common and non-convertible redeemable preferred stock to investors during a single round of financing. This third approach has been used with considerable success by venture firms large and small as an alternative to the traditional straight common or convertible preferred approach. Depending on a company's rate of growth and future capital needs, the combination common and non-convertible preferred has advantages over either the more traditional straight common or convertible preferred approaches.

The balance of this chapter discusses the interplay between common and preferred securities, examines the pros and cons of straight common and convertible preferred structures, and considers as an alternative approach the use of a common/non-convertible stock structure. Finally, the chapter considers how the common/non-convertible preferred structure affects the form a term sheet follows.

Straight Common or Convertible Preferred Structures

For discussion purposes, consider as a model a start-up company seeking its first venture round of $2 million. The management/shareholders, who own 100 percent of the company, value their holdings in the company at $3 million before the financing. Assuming this pre-financing valuation, after the financing the investors' $2 million interest will equal 40 percent of the equity; management will retain 60 percent of the equity; and the company will have a post-financing valuation of $5 million.

Typically, early-stage investments that involve friends and family of an entrepreneur or an early-stage management team will involve only common stock. The structure is simple, and the interests of the investors and management are clearly aligned. Both groups own common stock, and both are motivated to maximize its value. It has become customary for the first major round of professional venture investors to structure rounds of financing with convertible preferred stock. When an investment goes well, there is every motivation for convertible preferred stockholders to convert to common. If the model company cited above is sold or goes public at a $20 million value, the preferred holders would convert the 40 percent of the company they might hold in convertible preferred stock to common stock worth $8 million. The management team would have common stock worth $12 million.

On the downside, however, the use of preferred stock could give the investor certain protections and leave open the potential for less than optimal alignment between investors and management. The Liquidation Preference and Redemption sections of a term sheet specifically highlight the extent to which certain protective provisions can be afforded the convertible preferred investor. Assume the model company cited above does poorly and is sold for $4 million, $1 million less than the post-money valuation in the round. In a structure with straight common stock, management, owning 60 percent, would receive $2.4 million, while the investors would receive only $1.6 million, absorbing a loss of $400,000 on their investment. In such a scenario, the investors are likely to feel shortchanged, since management, responsible for the outcome, produced a meaningful gain for themselves and a loss for the investors. For this reason, a liquidation preference is typically attached to convertible preferred stock to provide first for complete return of capital to the preferred investors and then return of capital to common stockholders.

In the model cited above, the first $2 million of $4 million distributed in a sale would be distributed to the convertible stockholders. The next $2 million would be returned to common stockholders who would in this instance receive just $2 million of the original $3 million in value attributable to their common stock. The interests of preferred and common shareholders appear less aligned when the preferred require greater protection or, indeed, a guaranteed or minimum return of, say, one-and-one-half to two or more times. In such investor-favorable instances, the preferred investor could potentially receive all of the proceeds of a sale or liquidation. In our model, were the convertible preferred to require a return of two times and the company to be sold for $4 million, common shareholders would receive no value.

Case Study:
The Common and Non-convertible
Preferred Structure

With these two structures in mind, let's examine a third structure: straight common and straight, non-convertible, redeemable preferred. The explanation that follows and the analysis of the impact of this structure on management have been prepared with the assistance of Tom Claflin of Claflin Capital Management in Boston. Claflin Capital Management has managed some nine funds and, like other venture firms, has used this structure to partner successfully with portfolio companies in a majority of the deals the firm has financed. The common/non-convertible preferred structure is used in a minority of venture deals; however, it strives to align investors and management in a way that is different from how a convertible preferred typically acts.

The common/non-convertible preferred structure requires these two securities to be sold as a unit. In this structure the overall values are the same. If we assume the same example as cited above, in which a model company receives a pre-money valuation of $3 million and seeks to raise $2 million, the investors will, with the common/non-convertible preferred structure, also end up owning 40 percent of the company with their $2 million purchase. However, the investment is divided into two parts. Ninety percent of the investment, or $1.8 million, will purchase a non-convertible redeemable preferred, and 10 percent, or $200,000, will purchase 40 percent of the company's common stock. The 90/10 split is completely arbitrary; an 80/20 split has also been used with success. The ratio may change in later rounds.

While there is an implied overall post-financing value of $5 million based on $2 million of capital exchanged for 40 percent of the equity, this structure brings about a lower pre-money valuation while maintaining management's ownership percentage objective. The total value of the company's common stock is now $500,000 because 40 percent of the common was purchased for $200,000. When the $1.8 million of preferred is added to the $500,000 of common, the total value of the company becomes $2.3 million. This is the break-even value on the investment. If the company is sold for $2.3 million or more, the investors at least get their investment back. The break-even in this example is less than half of the $5 million valuation for a common stock deal.

In either the straight common stock or the convertible preferred stock structures, the investors would just get their cost back if the company were sold for $5 million. In the common/non-convertible preferred structure, if the company were sold for $5 million, the $1.8 million of preferred would be paid off the top, leaving $3.2 million for the common shareholders. The investors' 40 percent common holdings would be worth $1.28 million, bringing the total to $3.08 million, or a gain of 54 percent, compared to a break-even for either of the other two approaches.

In the case of a sale of the company for $20 million with the common/non-convertible preferred approach, the $1.8 million preferred comes off the top, and the remaining $18.2 million is divided among the shareholders. The investors' share of the common is $7.28 million, bringing their total to $9.08 million. This produces an extra $1.08 million, or a 14 percent better return than either the common or convertible preferred approach. In the traditional convertible preferred approach, the investors would have received $8 million for their effective 40 percent share as convertible preferred shareholders.

On the downside, the common/non-convertible preferred structure also works to the investors' advantage. The investors show a profit all the way down to a value of $2.3 million, where the investment reaches break-even. For example, at a $3 million valuation, $1.8 million of preferred comes off the top, leaving the investors' share of the common at $480,000 (40 percent of $1.2 million = $480,000). Thus, the investors would receive a total of $2.28 million if the company were sold for $3 million. Theoretically, for a value between $2.3 and $2 million, the convertible preferred approach is marginally better. However, at those levels, where management will not receive much from a sale, the preferred shareholders will likely be forced to give up some of their return to make the deal work.

Impact on Management

The common/non-convertible preferred approach is shown to be preferable from the investors' viewpoint. What is management's viewpoint? In the above example, management's return is potentially reduced as a function of the company's requirement to pay off the $1.8 million of preferred. In the case of a merger, the preferred definitely reduces management's share of the proceeds. If the company is sufficiently successful to pay off the preferred before being acquired, the negative impact to management is negligible. In the case of an IPO, as a practical matter, management's ownership value is not reduced by this structure. In this case the preferred is redeemed out of the offering proceeds and is lost in the noise level of the transaction.

Although the redeemable feature of the common/non-convertible preferred structure is a potential negative for management, there is a positive aspect, since the value of the common is driven down to one-tenth of the nominal value of a common or convertible preferred structure. This makes it somewhat easier to keep prices of the common lower for the benefit of pricing stock options for key management. To the extent that options are important to the management team, this can be a major advantage. Each equity percentage point has an option cost of $5,000 in the common/non-convertible preferred approach. It cost $50,000 for each percentage in the common stock or preferred approach.

Perhaps most importantly, the common/non-convertible preferred structure can benefit management by effecting a comparatively better valuation and less dilution for management. For example, if a common/non-convertible preferred structure is acceptable to investors at a $3 million pre-financing valuation, as in our company model, a convertible preferred might drop down to a $2.5 million pre-financing valuation and a common stock deal at a $1.5 million pre-financing valuation. The relative valuations of these three alternative structures should settle out where investors are indifferent as to which they would choose. The overall impact to the management as shareholders depends upon the ultimate exit value for the company.

Alignment of the Interests of Stakeholders

Perhaps the most obvious and strikingly important advantage to both management and investors of the common/non-convertible preferred structure is the clear alignment of interests the structure effects. Under such a structure, all participants hold common stock in the company. While the non-convertible preferred portion of an investor's holding is senior to common, and therefore likely to protect a substantial majority of the preferred investor's investment (90 percent in the above example), the remaining investment represents the majority of the investors' actual ownership in the company. As a result, the investor is, at the same time, keenly aware of the common goal of maximizing the value of common stock.

Alignment is further enforced by the simple fact that investors in the common/non-convertible preferred approach have paid one-tenth the price for their stock that would have been paid in a straight common stock structure. Consequently, they have a much higher probability of achieving a profit in their common stock investment sooner than in either of the other alternative approaches.

That the common/non-convertible preferred investors also hold non-convertible preferred has the subtle effect of motivating the non-convertible preferred to be more supportive when times get tough, as well as in the event of a follow-on financing.

When the situation becomes difficult, the preferred is more likely to be sacrificed to protect the investors' equity interest. This is a subtle, but significant, difference between the convertible preferred and the common/non-convertible preferred structures.

In the event of a follow-on financing, the common/non-convertible preferred stockholder is also likely to be more supportive of what might otherwise be a less attractive valuation to the pure convertible-preferred shareholder when the company is having considerable difficulty raising new capital. Consider our earlier example of a company that raised $2 million at a $3 million pre-money valuation. In this example, the original shareholders, in effect, hold 60 percent of the value in the company; the value of the company attributable to new investors represents 40 percent. For the purposes of this example, let's assume that were the financing in the form of a straight convertible security, 32,000 shares were issued at $62.50 to generate $2 million. If $2 million had been raised in the form of a bundle of common/non-convertible preferred securities, let's assume that 10 percent of the round, or $200,000, was issued in the form of 32,000 shares of common stock at $6.25, and 90 percent of the round, or $1.8 million, was issued in the form of 32,000 non-convertible preferred shares at $56.25.

Clearly, a follow-on investment in which a venture group of new investors proposes a new convertible preferred investment at $50 per share will create a different economic result, depending on whether the previous round had been in the form of convertible preferred stock or a combination of non-convertible preferred/common. Were the round in straight convertible preferred stock, the investor whose prior investment had been invested at $62.50 is forced to write-down his investment. The 32,000 shares valued at $62.50 per share need, in effect, to be re-priced on the books of the investor at $50.00. In either scenario, the new imputed value for the company is $4 million (80,000 shares at $50). A $2 million initial investment in convertible preferred would therefore need to be re-priced at $1.6 million on the books of the convertible preferred investor.

In contrast, the investors with common/non-convertible preferred securities would actually have little trouble with such an investment layered on top of their initial investment. Because the non-convertible preferred is non-convertible, its value must, in effect, be subtracted from the imputed value of the company before determining the value of the common. The non-convertible preferred/common investor actually would be able to justify a write-up of their overall investment by 34 percent, assuming at an imputed pre-financing value of $4 million. (80,000 shares x $50 = $4 million, less $1.8 million preferred, leaves $2.2 million for the common shareholders. 40 percent of $2.2 million = $880,000, + the $1.8 million preferred = $2.68 million, which, divided by the $2 million cost, = a 34 percent gain.)

Impact of Common and Non-convertible Preferred on Term Sheet Structure

Naturally the common/non-convertible preferred structure requires that the term sheet agreed to between investors and the company reflect a structure that is modified slightly as compared to the "standard" terms one would expect in a term sheet that involves conventional convertible preferred, as discussed in Chapter Three.

The nature of the common/non-convertible preferred structure contemplated in the financing will require a distinct form of language and structure for the term sheet that outlines such a financing. The distinct structure contemplated will first be outlined in the "New Securities Offered" section of the term sheet. In this section both non-convertible preferred and common shares to be purchased by the new investor need to be stipulated. The term sheet will also require significantly different language in the section "Rights, Preferences and Privileges of the Non-Convertible Preferred." In this section, the "Dividends" language will not necessarily contemplate dividends with respect to the non-convertible preferred stock. While a dividend may accrue, the non-convertible/common structure typically will assume that if a future financing or liquidity event does not transpire (eliminating buy-out of the non-convertible preferred), the non-convertible preferred will be bought out in full from company earnings during a stipulated time period. This will be clearly articulated in the "Liquidation" and "Redemption" clauses. Consequently, no "Conversion and Automatic Conversion" language will be required with respect to the non-convertible preferred, as the security is, by definition, non-convertible. "Dilution" clause language will also not contemplate dilution of the non-convertible preferred. Its value will, in effect, act like a debt instrument and not be subject to dilution. While the non-convertible preferred will require "Voting Rights," as well as "Protective Provisions" and "Special Board Approval Items" language, "Registration Rights" language will not pertain to the non-convertible preferred, only to the common.

3

DILUTION

In This Chapter . . .

The subject of dilution merits separate attention because it is, quite rightly, an extremely sensitive issue and one that needs careful consideration as companies consider their financing needs and the terms under which financings transpire. Indeed, as is explained in Chapter Three of *Term Sheets & Valuations,* "The single most important consideration when raising funds is anticipating how as a company grows new rounds of financing will affect the value of the shares of the company's existing shareholders." *(Page 54)*

A Sensitive Issue for Founders

I am always surprised when entrepreneurs are taken aback as institutional investors exercise the dilution protections afforded convertible preferred stock in a down-round – when the price per share in a round of financing is lower than the price per share in a prior round. The typical reaction of the entrepreneur is disbelief. Even when a company is doing well and meeting plan, a correction in the capital market may create a scenario in which new capital simply will not tolerate a flat round, a round at the same price as the prior round of financing, and will instead demand better terms. In one case, I witnessed an entrepreneur aghast that existing institutional investors would actually exercise their dilution protection provisions when a new round of financing resulted in little more than a 15 percent drop in company valuation. As I was in the fortunate position of setting terms for the round, I withheld my opinion on the matter. But given the fiduciary responsibility of the institutional investor to its limited partners, it is unlikely that an institutional investor would be willing or able to waive dilution provisions without receiving a written waiver from his or her limited partners. This is perhaps more a reflection of the nature of an institutionalized marketplace, and it is perhaps conceivable that a private investor could waive such provisions.

To elaborate on the gory facts and mechanics of dilution, I will lead by highlighting a few caveats. The extent to which investors may exercise their anti-dilution rights is negotiable. The term sheet and the terms interwoven into a company's charter are, in effect, potential negotiation points further down the road. The ownership position of management and management's willingness to work to ensure that a company meets its goals are clearly directly related. As management's enthusiasm and incentive to work to ensure an optimal outcome for a company become eroded by dilution, it is imperative that investors work to improve the balance and, where appropriate, consider additional options or incentives. When management's ownership position is perilously eroded as a result of dilution, the net effect of investors exercising their anti-dilution protections on one hand and creating additional options for management on the other hand is a loss of ownership percentage for common and preferred stockholders unable to leverage dilution protection.

This typically means that preferred stockholders in, for example, a Series A round who granted a company company-favorable anti-dilution terms may find themselves diluted without recourse when, after a Series B round in which Series B investors received investor-favorable dilution protection, a Series C round is priced below the Series B round. Similarly, angel investors and friends and family who purchased common stock may find themselves diluted under such circumstances. Ultimately though, dilution is often (friends and family aside) a relative matter, if you will excuse the pun. Common or Series A stock without dilution protection but purchased at a very low share price can maintain significant value in spite of a subsequent series of stock exercising dilution protection.

The Mechanics of Dilution

Investors who purchase preferred stock are concerned about future dilution and their ownership on a "common equivalent basis." This means that as a company adds rounds of preferred capital, unless there is some protection against dilution, the number of shares an investor owns will increasingly represent a smaller percentage of the company. For an investor to maintain the same or close to the same percentage of ownership, an investor either has to invest additional capital or ensure that he has some form of anti-dilution protection. What anti-dilution protection brings, in effect, is a mechanism that allows an investor to continue to hold an equal or close to equal percentage of ownership in a company without requiring the investor to commit more capital.

The mechanics are captured in a company's corporate charter or "Certificate of Incorporation." This document should capture the rights associated with common and preferred stock and outline the mechanics of how dilution protections are to be handled. Because dilution is such a central concern to investors, the extent to which classes of preferred stock need to be consulted, should the company want to issue additional shares or amend its charter, is a central point of a term sheet negotiation and is captured in the corporate charter. A preferred class of stock may also require and stipulate in the charter such elements as the requirement of a majority approval by the stockholders of that class of stock for any amendments to the bylaws of the corporation to be made, indebtedness beyond $500,000, for example, or any further issue of securities.

The preferred equity section of the charter will include an entire section devoted to the subject of "Conversion" and specifically to how conversion should be handled in the event of dilution. In some documents the applicable subsections are titled "Right to Convert" and "Adjustment of Conversion Price Upon Issuance of Additional Shares of Common Stock."

One core concept that one must understand to understand the mechanics of dilution is the concept of "on an as converted basis." The "conversion price" of preferred stock is the price at which one share of preferred will convert to common or be treated as if converted to common for purposes of ownership percentage calculations and liquidation. It is easy to understand that if a mechanism exists for the investor to be able to have the "conversion price" adjusted in the event of certain occurrences, the investor ultimately holds the right to adjust the number of shares of common into which his or her preferred security can convert and that this right adjusts depending on how the conversion price is adjusted. As a practical matter, the conversion section will initially set the "conversion price" of the preferred stock at the price at which the stock was purchased.

While the conversion price typically begins as the price of the share at purchase, the conversion price will be adjusted if a company subsequently issues additional securities, and the rights associated with that existing preferred stock provide for an adjustment to its conversion price in the event of dilution when a subsequent class of preferred stock is issued. If a new class of stock has an issue price below the price of a prior class of stock and the rights of a prior class of stock provide for anti-dilution protection, the corporate charter will need to be amended and restated and the conversion price associated with the prior class of stock adjusted. In effect, the "conversion price" is adjusted downward to compensate for the effect of dilution.

Full-ratchet Provisions

The full-ratchet is the most investor-favorable of anti-dilution protections available to the investor. With good reason, it makes the hair of the entrepreneur stand on end and sends a shiver up the spine. In the case of a full-ratchet, the conversion price is adjusted to ensure that the new price factors in the total amount of capital invested and preserves the full percentage ownership of the preferred. Consider the simple table below, which captures the complete economic effect and result to the cap table of a company.

	Series A Price & Series A Conversion Price	Common Equiv. Shares Out- standing	Owner- ship %	Series B Price & Series A&B Conversion Price	Common Equivalent Shares Out- standing	Owner- ship %
Options		1000	33%		1000	20%
Common		1000	33%		1000	20%
Series A	$2	1000	33%	$1	2000	40%
Series B				$1	1000	20%

Clearly, the repercussions of a full-ratchet are most serious for common stockholders and options recipients. These are the two sets of stakeholders who typically will get diluted, along with any class of preferred stock that may not have such protections. Hence the conundrum for companies that are able to receive high pre-money valuations early in their lives. The entrepreneur may think this is a risk worth taking; however, valuations that are prematurely high in early rounds can adversely affect the marketability of a company in a later round. Investors who come to the table may sense that the management and its previous investors had lofty and inappropriate expectations and that, as a result, management may be difficult to work with or to rely on when it comes to future performance. The economic consequences of a down round, and a full-ratchet in particular, can also be devastating for existing shareholders whose impatience and soured demeanor can create a less than welcoming environment for new investors.

Weighted-average Dilution

In the case of a weighted average anti-dilution, the conversion price is adjusted on a weighted average basis and therefore only partially compensates for dilution.

An adjustment to the conversion price therefore has a direct bearing on the number of common shares for which preferred shares can be exchanged when a preferred shareholder chooses to convert to common stock. The number of shares of common stock into which the preferred stock is convertible will be determined by dividing the price of the preferred stock by the conversion price in effect at the time of conversion.

The calculation below outlines a real-life example of how the conversion price of a preferred class of stock is adjusted using the weighted-average anti-dilution formula. In the example, a new round of preferred stock is issued at $9.71. The original conversion price of the prior Series D preferred stock is adjusted from $12.82 to $12.1794 to compensate for a down-round and lower pricing.

Adjustment to Conversion Price Based on
Weighted-Average Calculation

Common	577,500	
Series A	303,282	
Series B	152,594	
Series C	116,981	
Options	81,952	
Total Outstanding	1,232,309	
	1,537,497	# shares outstanding assuming Series E at Series C price
	1,541,269	# shares outstanding assuming Series E at Series E price
Series C purchase price	9.830	
Series C conversion price (1,537,497/1,541,269) x 9.83	9.806	New equivalent weighted average price per share for Series C
	1,466,318	# shares outstanding assuming Series E at Series D price
	1,541,269	# shares outstanding assuming Series E at Series E price
Series D purchase price	12.820	
Series D conversion price (1,466,318/1,541,269) x 12.82	12.197	New equivalent weighted average price per share for Series D

Narrow-based vs. Broad-based Weighted-average Anti-dilution

When weighted average anti-dilution protection is discussed, it is critical to know how to differentiate between the various forms that exist. Whereas full-ratchet anti-dilution protection is comparatively straightforward, weighted-average dilution formulas typically leave open the possibility of broader interpretation and definition. The weighted-average dilution protection can be either broad-based or narrow-based.

Consider the table below, which outlines the effects of a narrow-based versus a broad-based interpretation of a company's cap table. In the most capital-strained periods, the most investor-favorable term is narrow-based anti-dilution protection because the narrow-based interpretation typically calculates only issued options as part of the option pool and the total capital structure. Doing so ensures that the investor's position on a percentage basis is greater. This interpretation is typically referred to as an "East Coast" term.

The "California" interpretation is known more commonly as "broad-based." Under this interpretation, the entire options pool – options issued, as well as those reserved to be issued – is included in the interpretation of the cap table. As such, the preferred is seen to own less of the company, and any future options issued are not perceived as being at all dilutive because they have already been factored into the interpretation of the capital structure of the company.

In the most investor-favorable circumstance, where a narrow-based interpretation of the capital structure is employed as a company issues any options beyond those issued at time of financing, a weighted average anti-dilution formula might be applied to adjust the conversion price of preferred shares to compensate for the dilutive effect of issuing more options.

Common Percent Ownership

	Equiv. Shares Out-standing	Ownership % Narrow-based	Ownership % Broad-based
Options issued	1000	33%	25%
Options reserved	1000	N/A	25%
Common	1000	33%	25%
Series A	1000	33%	25%

4

STOCK OPTIONS AND THEIR EFFECT ON CAPITAL STRUCTURE

In This Chapter . . .

Competitive stock option programs are an integral part of a private or public organization's compensation policy. As such, stock option programs are a significant part of a company's capital structure and an important part of the valuation discussion and analysis that investors undergo.

As companies expand their headcount, their cash flow and, typically, capital needs increase for some period. Attendant with any increase in headcount presumably is the need to increase a company's option pool. The need for any increase in capital not only places dilutive pressure on a company's overall capital structure, but also erodes the percentage holding of employees who are members of a company's stock option program.

Balancing Financing Needs with Competitive Best Practices

The extent to which an option pool can be a significant source of discussion and consternation is directly tied to cost of equity capital for a company. Options are dilutive to investors. Whereas founders and angel investors often hold important positions in the capital structure of any early-stage company, a company's capital needs and the valuation tied to any equity investment assume significant needs in terms of options and compensation going forward. Few companies can run, scale, and generate handsome returns to investors without increasing their headcount and management team over time.

Companies that can point to compelling investment opportunities and command the interest of strong, established, and experienced equity investors should be able to agree to reasonable expectations on the part of prospective investors about the size of the future option pool and to what extent it will need to grow. The elements that any competent analysis of an option program need to have taken into account include defining the competitive market for compensation – specifically, the cash and equity components. Established accounting and law firms with a strong venture practice can be as strong a source of information as compensation consultants. Key to a company's success in both generating financing and remaining competitive is a strong commitment to reviewing current equity holdings of key management and assessing them in the context of the competitive marketplace. Investors will want to see a stock option grant strategy in place and are likely to make some quite definitive assumptions of their own regarding the size and growth of the option pool during the life of their investment in the company.

It is important to note that some investors – and strategic investors, in particular – may not realize market norms for option grants in small, high-risk companies. In many cases, their more conservative assumptions can pose a real challenge for management teams that are not compensated well enough, but realize that only after precedents have been set. Employees, too, have a lot to learn about stock option levels, but a board should assume that eventually employees will have to be closely aligned with the marketplace or, otherwise, should be prepared to compensate managers mostly in cash.

Employee expectations with regard to the number of options vary significantly. Interestingly enough, many employees are satisfied with a specific number of shares in a company without placing value on how that number of shares may translate in percentage terms. It may seem logical enough for an employee to assume, if the most recent price of preferred stock was $1, the employee is awarded 250,000 shares of options, and investors expect to sell the company for $4 per share, that his or her shares could be worth $1 million. What employees often lose sight of is the amount of capital a company may require, as conditions change, to meet its goals and how many additional shares may need to be issued. Whereas astute investors protect themselves from dilution through the use of preferred stock, employees are diluted as additional stock is issued, unless they are awarded additional options along the way.

Some employees focus instead on percentage ownership. There are obvious pitfalls to emphasizing or agreeing to employment contracts that tie options grants to a fixed percentage ownership in a company. This becomes a significant liability and a continued drag on the options pool as a company seeks to raise additional capital. But it is appropriate to consider awards set against some percentage benchmark for senior levels of management. I have seen wide ranges in ownership in many companies that are not yet profitable. The range for CEOs, some of whom own founders shares, can vary from 3 percent to 13 percent and for CFOs from 1 percent to 2.5 percent. I have seen the range for key executives, including vice president and director level staff, from .5 percent to 1.5 percent. Often geographic regions will have their own unique profiles, and so it is appropriate to ask experienced executive search professionals, attorneys, and accountants for a sense of the local market when it comes to options.

Dilution and the Protections Investors May Require

Investors are fully aware of the dilutive effect of a financing on an option pool. VC investors especially are typically keenly aware of market parameters and standards regarding stock option compensation. Strategic investors may not be as up to date as they are more familiar with options plans in much larger companies. It is not uncommon, therefore, that strict expectations for the size and profile of a stock option pool will be set at the time of a financing, enumerated and outlined in a section titled "Reserved Shares." Consider the passage below from a term sheet related to a financing:

Reserved Shares:	The Company currently has or will have 3,000,000 shares of Common reserved for issuance to directors, officers, employees, and consultants upon the exercise of outstanding and future options (the "Reserved Shares").
	The Reserved Shares will be issued from time to time to directors, officers, employees and consultants of the Company under such arrangements, contracts or plans as are recommended by management and approved by the Board, provided that without the unanimous consent of the directors elected solely by the Preferred, the vesting of any such shares (or options therefore) issued to any such person shall not be at a rate in excess of 25% per annum from the date of issuance. Unless subsequently agreed to the contrary by the investors, any issuance of shares in excess of the Reserved Shares will be a dilutive event requiring adjustment of the conversion price as provided above and will be subject to the investors' first offer right as described below. Holders of Reserved Shares will be required to execute stock restriction agreements with the Company providing for certain restrictions on transfer and for the Company's right of first refusal.
Right of First Offer for Purchase of New Securities:	So long as any of the Preferred is outstanding, if the Company proposes to offer any shares for the purpose of financing its business (other than Reserved Shares, shares issued in the acquisition of another company, or shares offered to the public pursuant to an underwritten public offering), the Company will first offer a portion of such shares to the holders of Preferred so as to enable them to maintain their percentage interest in the Company.

71

The purpose of the "Reserved Shares" clause in a term sheet is to set in place certain expectations that define exactly how large an option pool will grow before those preferred shareholders may benefit from any protection outlined in the clause. In the example above, the investors proposing the term sheet outlined that the financing would assume that up to 3,000,000 shares of common could be reserved "for issuance to directors, officers, employees, and consultants upon the exercise of outstanding and future options." The clause clearly places a ceiling on the number of shares of common that can be issued upon exercise of options by these constituencies. The clause goes on to detail that unless the investors agree otherwise, any issuance of shares as a result of additional options will need to result in full anti-dilution protection and an adjustment to the conversion price of the shares held by the investors who propose this round of financing. The clause clearly states, "Unless subsequently agreed to the contrary by the investors, any issuance of shares in excess of the Reserved Shares will be a dilutive event requiring adjustment of the conversion price as provided above and will be subject to the investors' first offer right as described below." The "Right of First Offer for Purchase of New Securities" language that follows the "Reserved Shares" clause in effect proposes that the investors proposing the financing be allowed to maintain their ownership percentage and in effect purchase more shares in the company if additional options issued result in the need to issue more than 3,000,000 shares of common stock.

The full range of an investor's potential tools in stock incentive planning includes the ability to require founders to bind some number of shares of common stock under a stock restriction agreement. In so doing, an existing ownership position can be treated as restricted stock that is earned over a period of years. This in effect resets the clock on the stock founders may own at the time of an early-stage financing. When market conditions and company progress indicate to investors that founders' option packages are either too rich or are in line with the market but owned outright, requiring that these individuals agree to extend the time frame they will need to work to fully own stock is one mechanism that can keep employees motivated, but not require a company to issue more options to do so.

Director and Advisory Board Member Compensation – The Hidden Costs of Added Value

Directors, whether they are independent directors with industry expertise or VCs with investment expertise, can be a source of significant added value to a company. The worst form of directors are the "pigeons": as the analogy goes, they fly in to a board meeting, eat lunch, crap all over a company, and then fly off again, only to reappear for the next board meeting. Active, value-adding directors serve on board committees – compensation, audit, and planning committees, for example – and their effectiveness is a direct result of their ability to apply experience and specific expertise in finance or operations to their roles on the board and on the committees to which they have been assigned.

Many entrepreneurs scratch their heads at the value certain kinds of directors, specifically VCs, may play as a company evolves. I remember being particularly proud when a founder of a fast-growing and successful enterprise software company whose board I served on turned to me at a board meeting and said with a degree of humility and excitement that he finally realized how valuable VC directors were to the company. The company had weathered a soul-searching period of flat revenues, and the VC directors had rallied the company's board to adopt a dynamic compensation program that had proved particularly effective at another one of their portfolio companies. Through focus and better allocation of resources, the other company had managed to increase its revenues over the previous year by a factor of ten and, quite appropriately, energized management with generous incentive bonuses.

I am not quite certain whether it ever impressed the founder that VC directors do not typically personally receive stock options in their role as directors. In many pre-IPO companies, independent directors and employees are the only groups serving on boards who receive director stock options. When the decision is made to award financial investors with stock options as compensation for their role as company directors, their respective partnerships typically require those shares to be assigned to their partnerships and not received personally. The driver behind this requirement is the management agreement between VCs and their limited partners or investors. When serving on the board of a private company, VCs typically are required to deduct compensation they receive for services they would otherwise be paid for under their management agreement from the fees they charge their limited partners. To receive fees from investors and to be paid stock for serving as a director of a private company in which a VC's fund has invested is viewed as "double-dipping" and an improper alignment of interest.

VCs are, however, likely to be able to receive options personally when they serve on the board of a public company, even when that company is part of a VC's limited partner's portfolio. The rationale in this instance is that, in serving on a public company, the VC accepts a higher degree of liability personally and for this liability should be personally compensated.

To illustrate the typical costs of attracting and retaining competent board members, I have consulted Stephen Fowler at BoardSeat, a retained search firm that focuses exclusively on board director and advisor searches. The group takes as its primary focus public and venture-backed companies and conducts surveys because of the considerable uncertainty of many companies, investors, and professional advisors about market rates for compensation of board directors and advisory board members of venture-backed companies. In compiling survey data, they take the opportunity to ask key questions about how venture-backed companies administer their boards and advisory boards.

A copy of BoardSeat's first set of survey results is featured as an appendix of this book and represents a comprehensive study of the administration and compensation of boards and advisory boards for private companies. According to BoardSeat, the data from the survey includes feedback from 100 companies, the majority of which have received substantial backing from tier-one venture firms. Validating the value of this information, many tier-one VC firms, according to BoardSeat, purchase their reports, including Apax, General Atlantic, Highland, Kleiner Perkins, Lightspeed, Mayfield, NEA, Norwest, Redpoint, Sevin Rosen, Sierra Ventures, TVM, and Versant. The company can be consulted at www.boardseat.com.

BoardSeat sent a questionnaire concerning board director and advisory board practices and compensation to 400 private venture capital backed companies, the majority of which had received more than $10 million in venture funding. According to BoardSeat, most companies had received backing by tier-one venture capital firms. Perhaps not surprisingly, as companies raised more money, their board of directors tended to get bigger, a trend typically attributable to the addition of constituencies and new sources of guidance as a company expands. BoardSeat claims the average board size for companies that had raised less than $10 million is 5.3 members; whereas, the average board size for companies that had raised more than $50 million is 6.7 members.

Perhaps more interesting to entrepreneurs is BoardSeat's data reflecting compensation for directors and advisors. For companies that raised under $10 million, BoardSeat reports the mean percentage of shares granted to independent board directors per year is between 0.07 percent and 0.08 percent of the fully diluted shares. The number drops to less than 0.05 percent for companies that raised over $50 million, reflecting the appropriate ratio of compensation to a significantly larger number of shares typically outstanding for companies that have raised such large amounts of capital.

While the role of an advisory board in my experience varies depending upon industry and company, more than half the companies BoardSeat surveyed had some type of advisory board and were more likely to have one in the early stages of development than in the more mature stages. Interestingly, the compensation received by directors as compared to advisors was predictably skewed in favor of directors. BoardSeat found that companies that had raised less than $10 million pay advisors 0.043 percent per year per advisor on average, a number that BoardSeat concludes equals about half that paid to directors. Companies that had raised more than $50 million paid advisors about one quarter the number of shares paid to board directors.

5

Flat Rounds and Down-rounds: Term Sheets as Roadmaps

In This Chapter . . .

This chapter features a term sheet for an expansion-stage company that, by necessity, needed to raise expansion capital and did so in a down market. The result is a series of terms designed to both set the stage for a new round of financing and ensure that the new class of security, in this case a Series E, is adequately protected from future down-rounds. The names of the company and the venture firms represented in the term sheet, as well as the exact shareholding numbers, capital structure, and board dynamics have been changed to respect confidentiality.

Several aspects of this term sheet are unique to the company and to a down-round, and they should be highlighted. While the term sheet is analyzed and discussed in the first part of this chapter, it can be found in complete form in the last eight pages of the chapter; please cross-reference as you read.

Multiple Classes of Preferred Stock and Implications in a Flat- or Down-Round Financing

As is outlined in the "Current Securities" section, the company has five classes of shares at the time of the proposed financing – four preferred and one common. In this case, the shares of the Series A and Series B preferred stock are held by wealthy individual investors close to the founders. The shares of the Series C and Series D preferred stock are held by one single institutional investor. Quite typically, the majority of the common stock is held by the founder of the company.

The term sheet contemplates a new class of security, Series E. The company in this example is clearly moving its way quickly down the alphabet and will quite likely entertain a subsequent and final round of expansion capital before becoming cash-flow break-even. In a tight capital market, the terms of the round and of this proposed Series E do not in many ways reflect an "also ran" class of preferred security. The proposed class of stock in this flat-round is very much like a Series A and has attached to it more restrictive terms than those associated with any prior preferred round. Psychologically, the round is very much a down-round in its effect. The term sheet proposes seniority in terms of liquidation preference over all other securities. It also proposes an adjustment of the board to align it more closely with the most recent classes of preferred stock and specifically this Series E.

In many ways, the story behind this term sheet is nonetheless positive. The company was able to raise money at a challenging time, though its investors had to adjust their expectations and accept that the company's business model had required more time and more capital than had been anticipated.

Serial classes of preferred stock as part of the capital structure therefore do not necessarily indicate failure. For companies that have consistently raised rounds of financing at successively higher valuations because of an impressive record of progress and superior value creation, each new class of security will represent an appropriate upward adjustment to price and presumably less risk to the investor. Particularly as a company generates increasing momentum and moves closer to cash flow break-even, the protections of each subsequent round are either likely to mirror previous preferred rounds and protect those rounds *pari-passu* (on an equal and shared footing) or are likely to command less stringent and investor-favorable protections. In short, the capital raise may actually be a Series E at a price that is higher than all subsequent rounds and, in a company-friendly environment, not attach many terms that are investor-favorable.

Resetting the Clock

In the case of the company whose term sheet is featured in this chapter, the combination of a tough capital market and failure to be cash flow positive has required a new round of financing in the form of a Series E Preferred that, in effect, "resets" the clock and acts more like an early-stage Series A or Series B security than the type of Series E that might be associated with a later-stage company.

The single institutional investor previously divided its investment between two series of preferred stock, the Series C and the Series D, as a result of an initial agreement between the investor and the company at the time of the Series C, which stipulated that the investor would do so if the company achieved certain milestones. The Series D class of preferred stock afforded the company a step-up in valuation over the Series C, and the company did achieve its milestones. What the company failed to anticipate was the extent to which achieving its milestones would consume all of its capital and fail to be compelling enough to raise a final round of capital at a significantly higher valuation and on improved terms to the Series D.

The Series C preferred stock had assumed a $10 million pre-money valuation. The Series D preferred stock had previously valued the company at $13.5 million pre-money. As $1.5 million was invested in the Series D, the post-money valuation after the Series D was $15 million. The Series E would assume a pre-money valuation of $15 million.

What is unique about the capital structure of the company, and not represented in the term sheet, is that the Series A and Series B preferred stock holds nothing more than one times liquidation preference and no anti-dilution protection. The Series C and Series D preferred stock, however, holds weighted-average anti-dilution protection. In this case, the $15 million pre-money valuation proposed for the Series E is a flat-round when compared to the Series D preferred round. Even though the pre-money valuation proposed for the Series E round is the same as the post-money valuation for the Series D round, the Series E round is still slightly dilutive. Once the full $5 million contemplated in the term sheet for the Series E is raised, 25 percent of the company is sold.

From a liquidation preference and dilution perspective, the Series A and Series B are therefore more closely aligned with the common than the Series C and Series D. In contrast, the anti-dilution provisions as proposed in the term sheet for the proposed Series E are the same as the powers held by the Series C and D. It could be argued that the institutional and venture fund money represented in the term sheet and under the Series C, D, and E will be more closely aligned with one another because of its similar liquidation preference and perspective.

There are nonetheless important differences between the Series E and all prior classes of stock. First, the Series E under the terms proposed would retain the right to two times liquidation preference over all other stock in the company. The Series E calls for receiving $20, or twice the value of the initial investment in each Series E share, in the event of liquidation before all other shareholders. If the Series E receives more than $20 per share on an as-converted-to-common basis in liquidation, the Series E would obviously convert to common, and this liquidation preference would not be exercised. In some cases, preferred investors will demand that they receive a liquidation preference and then receive a return of capital alongside all shareholders on an as-converted-to-common basis. This is called a participating preferred. It has the effect of double-dipping. A participating preferred is not contemplated in this term sheet.

The second and materially different right or power proposed by the Series E, as compared to all prior classes of stock, is reconfiguration of the company's board and management team. It is not uncommon that a condition to a new round of financing may be the hire of additional talent. It is also quite typical that a new class of security requires board representation. The term sheet calls for restructuring the board to represent more balance between the common and its affiliates and the institutional investors.

The company's board at the time the term sheet was proposed comprised five directors, with two seats held by the preferred A and B (voting together), one seat held by the preferred C and D (voting together), and two seats held by the common.

The term sheet proposes the board be expanded to seven. While the proposed structure preserves the two common seats controlled by the founder, the board profile and balance, as proposed, would change significantly. Under the proposed structure, the preferred A and B (voting together) reduce their number of seats from two to one; the preferred C and D (voting together) continue to hold one seat; the Series E holds one seat; and an independent director and a new CEO are each allocated seats.

The way the company would make the transition from a five-person to a seven-person board is also stipulated. While not stipulated, the assumption behind the selection process is that the institutional and venture investors compose one group, and that the common and Series A and B preferred compose a second group, and that the groups need to be in agreement. Once the CEO is selected, the final configuration of the board moves significant influence into the hands of the new CEO and the independent director.

The "Expenses" section is not unusual. The company prefers to retain its counsel to draft the documents for the proposed round. This is reasonable because in this case the company's counsel drafted the documents for the Series C and D preferred rounds, and the terms of the Series E preferred round are not significantly different from those prior rounds. Presumably, drafting for a Series E preferred round would require less work for company counsel and therefore less cost to the company. Investors in the Series E round nevertheless are entitled to their own independent counsel and customarily require that expenses charged by their counsel to review documents related to the round be reimbursed by the company upon closing of the round. For this reason, the lead investor in the Series E has required that the company reimburse expenses of its counsel up to an agreed cap of $30,000. While counsel to the investor is unlikely to agree to a hard cap, there is often some understanding established as to an approximate cost. In this way the company is able to maintain consistency with regard to drafting its shareholder documents, while the new investors are able to retain a degree of influence over review and acceptance of documents.

The final passage serves to protect both parties and reiterates that the term sheet does not represent a legally binding obligation on either party. From the perspective of both parties, the goodwill established between the parties will motivate them to work toward a closing. The disclaimer clause is designed to preserve the rights of investors and members of the company in the event of a materially negative or positive change to the business of the company.

Case Study:
Company, Inc.

Summary of Terms for Proposed Private
Placement of Series E Preferred Stock

Issuer: Company, Inc. ("Company")

Current Securities: 200,000 shares of Series A Preferred Stock ("Series A Preferred"), 200,000 shares of Series B Preferred Stock ("Series B Preferred"), 250,000 shares of Series C Preferred Stock ("Series C Preferred"), 250,000 shares of Series D Preferred Stock ("Series D Preferred"), 500,000 shares of Common Stock ("Common") and 100,000 shares of Common reserved for issuance pursuant to Stock Option Plan.

Amount of Investment: Not less than $3.5 million, and not to exceed $5.0 million, of which at least $1.5 million will be from Venture Firm or its affiliates.

Proposed Initial Closing Date: January 1, 2002.

Type of Security: Series E Preferred Stock ("Series E Preferred"),

Number of Shares: Not less than 350,000 and not to exceed 500,000.

Price per Share: $10.0 ("Original Purchase Price"). Based on an approximately $15.0 million valuation of current securities.

Rights, Preferences, Privileges and Restrictions of Preferred: (1) <u>Dividend Provisions</u>: The holders of outstanding Series E Preferred will be entitled to receive dividends in any fiscal year, when, as and if declared by the Board of Directors.

No dividend will be paid on the shares of any class of securities junior to the Series E Preferred unless dividends representing an equal amount on a per share equivalence basis shall have been paid on all the outstanding shares of the Series E Preferred. No shares of Common will be repurchased by the Company except for (i) unvested shares repurchased from former employees at their original purchase price, or (ii) if approved by a majority of the Board of Directors (including at least one director designated by the holders of Series E Preferred), shares repurchased by the Company from the holders thereof pursuant to rights of first refusal granted to the Company and to holders of Series E Preferred.

(2) <u>Liquidation Preference</u>: In the event of the liquidation or winding up of the Company, the holders of Series E Preferred will be entitled to receive, in preference to the holders of the Series A Preferred, the Series B Preferred, the Series C Preferred and the Series D Preferred (collectively, the "Existing Preferred") and Common an amount ("Liquidation Amount") equal to $20.00. After the Liquidation Amount has been paid, the holders of the Series C Preferred and Series D Preferred will be entitled to receive from the remaining assets, the applicable liquidation preference, if any, as is currently established in the Company's Charter. Thereafter, the holders of Common and the Series A Preferred and the Series B Preferred will be entitled to receive the remaining assets, with the Series A Preferred and the Series B Preferred being treated as equivalent to the number of shares of Common into which it is convertible. A consolidation or merger of the Company or sale of all or substantially all of its assets will be deemed to be a liquidation or winding up for purposes of the liquidation preference.

(3) <u>Conversion</u>: A holder of Series E Preferred will have the right to convert the Series E Preferred, at the option of the holder, at any time, into shares of Common. The total number of shares of Common into which the Series E Preferred may be converted initially will be determined by dividing the Original Purchase Price by the conversion price. The initial conversion price will be the Original Purchase Price. The conversion price will be subject to adjustment as provided in paragraph (5) below.

(4) <u>Automatic Conversion</u>: The Series E Preferred will be automatically converted into Common, at the then applicable conversion price, in the event of an underwritten public offering of shares of the Common at a public offering

price per share that is not less than 2-1/2 times the Series E Preferred Original Purchase Price (as adjusted for stock splits or recapitalizations) in an offering of not less than $20,000,000, or upon the vote of the holders of not less than sixty percent (60%) of the then outstanding shares the Series E Preferred, voting separately.

(5) <u>Anti-dilution Provisions</u>: If the Company issues additional shares (other than the Reserved Shares described under "Reserved Shares" below and for other customary exceptions) at a purchase price less than the applicable conversion price, the conversion price of the Series E Preferred will be reduced on a weighted average formula basis to diminish the effect of such dilutive issuance on the Series E Preferred.

(6) <u>Voting Rights</u>: Except with respect to election of directors and certain protective provisions, the holders of the Existing Preferred and the Series E Preferred (collectively, the "Preferred") will have the right to that number of votes equal to the number of shares of Common issuable upon conversion of the Preferred. Election of directors and the protective provisions will be as described under "Board Representation and Meetings" and "Protective Provisions", respectively, below.

(7) <u>Protective Provisions</u>: Consent of the holders of at least sixty percent (60%) of the Series E Preferred will be required for (i) any sale by the Company of substantially all of its assets, (ii) any merger of the Company with another entity (iii) any liquidation or winding up of the Company, (iv) any amendment of the Company's charter or bylaws, (v) issuance of any equity securities or securities exchangeable or exercisable for, or convertible into equity securities, other than Reserved Shares, unless such issuance has been approved by a majority of the Board of Directors, including not less than one of two directors elected by holders of the Series E Preferred, (vi) incurrence of indebtedness in excess of $500,000 in the aggregate, or (vii) certain other actions materially affecting the Series E Preferred.

(8) <u>Redemption</u>: On each of January 1, 2007, April 15, 2008 and April 15, 2009, at the request of holders of not

less than 60% of the Series E Preferred, the Company will redeem one-third of the Series E Preferred originally issued by paying in cash per share the Original Purchase Price, plus any declared but unpaid dividends payable on the Series E Preferred.

Information Rights:

So long as any of the Series E Preferred investors own at least 2% of the Company's issued and outstanding capital stock, the Company will deliver to each such investor annual, quarterly and, monthly financial statements (if requested), monthly management reports (if requested), annual budgets and other information reasonably requested by an investor.

Registration Rights:

(1) <u>Demand Rights</u>: If, at any time not earlier than the earlier of (i) January 1, 2003 or (ii) 180 days after the effective date of the first registration statement filed by the Company covering an underwritten offering of any capital stock to the general public (but not within 6 months of the effective date of a registration), investors holding at least 40% of the Common issued or issuable upon conversion of the Series E Preferred request that the Company file a Registration Statement covering shares of the Common issued or issuable upon conversion of the Series E Preferred, the Company will use its best efforts to cause such shares to be registered.

The Company will not be obligated to effect more than two registrations (other than on Form S-3) under these demand right provisions.

(2) <u>Registrations on Form S-3</u>: Holders of Common issued or issuable upon conversion of the Series E Preferred will have the right to require the Company to file an unlimited number of Registration Statements on Form S-3 (or any equivalent successor form) (but not more than twice in any twelve-month period) provided the anticipated aggregate offering price in each registration on Form S-3 will exceed $750,000.

(3) <u>Piggy-Back Registration</u>: The investors will be entitled to "piggy-back" registration rights on registrations of the Company, subject to the right of the Company and its under-writers to reduce in view of market conditions the

number of shares of the investors proposed to be registered to not less than 30% of the total number of shares in the offering.

(4) <u>Registration Expenses</u>: The registration expenses (exclusive of underwriting discounts and commissions) of all of the registrations under paragraphs (1), (2) and (3) above will be borne by the Company.

(5) <u>Transfer of Registration Rights</u>: The registration rights may be transferred to a transferee who acquires at least 50,000 shares of Common issued or issuable on conversion of the Series E Preferred. Transfer of registration rights to a partner or shareholder of any investor will be without restriction as to minimum shareholding.

(6) <u>Other Registration Provisions</u>: Other provisions will be contained in the Investor Rights Agreement with respect to registration rights as are reasonable, including cross-indemnification, the Company's ability to delay the filing of a demand registration for a period of not more than 90 days in certain circumstances, the agreement by the investors (if requested by the under-writers in a public offering) not to sell any unregistered Common they hold for a period of 180 days following the effective date of the Registration Statement of the Company's initial public offering, the period of time in which the Registration Statement will be kept effective, the circumstances under which the Company will not be required to register an investor's shares, underwriting arrangements and the like.

(7) <u>No Registration of Preferred</u>: The registration rights set forth herein apply only to the Common and the Company will never be obligated to register any of the Series E Preferred.

Use of Proceeds: The proceeds from the sale of the Series E Preferred will be used for working capital and general corporate purposes as determined by the Board of Directors.

Board Representation and Meetings: The charter will provide that the authorized number of directors is seven. The Series A and the B (voting together) will elect one director, Series C and D (voting together) will elect one director, the Series E Preferred (voting as a class) will elect two directors until such time as the Company has hired a Chief Executive Officer ("CEO"), one of which will be held by a nominee of VC Firm, the Common (voting as a class) will elect two directors, and following the hiring of the CEO and his election to the Board as described below, a majority of the members of the Board will elect an independent director with industry expertise. Upon the hiring of a CEO, the nominee of the Series E Preferred which is not a representative of VC Firm will resign and the CEO shall be appointed a director of the Company. The Board will meet at least quarterly. Reasonable expenses related to the attendance of board meetings by the Series E director[s] designated by the E Preferred will be reimbursed by the Company. The bylaws will provide, in addition to any provisions required by law, that any two directors or holders of at least 25% of the Preferred may call a meeting of the Board. The Board shall have audit and compensation committees, and one Series E director shall be appointed to each. D&O Insurance for $5mm will be purchased by the Company for benefit of directors.

Key Person Insurance: $1,000,000 on the founder with the proceeds payable to the Company.

Right of First Offer for Purchase of New Securities: So long as any of the Preferred is outstanding, if the Company proposes to offer any shares for the purpose of financing its business (other than Reserved Shares, shares issued in the acquisition of another company, or shares offered to the public pursuant to an underwritten public offering and other customary exceptions), the Company will first offer a portion of such shares to the holders of Preferred and holders of Common so as to enable them to maintain their percentage interest in the Company.

Stockholders' Agreement: The Series E Preferred investors shall become parties to a Co-Sale Agreement with certain "Founders" named therein and the holders of the Preferred. In addition, all current and future holders of Common Stock shall execute agreements with the Company and investors containing comparable terms.

Reserved Shares:

The Company currently has or will have 100,000 shares of Common reserved for issuance to directors, officers, employees, and consultants upon the exercise of outstanding and future options (the "Reserved Shares").

The Reserved Shares will be issued from time to time to directors, officers, employees and consultants of the Company under such arrangements, contracts or plans as are recommended by management and approved by the Board, provided that without the unanimous consent of the directors designated solely by the Preferred, the vesting of any such shares (or options therefor) issued to any such person shall not be at a rate in excess of 33-1/3% per annum from the date of issuance. Unless subsequently agreed to the contrary by the investors, any issuance of shares in excess of the Reserved Shares will be a dilutive event requiring adjustment of the conversion price as provided above and will be subject to the investors' first offer right as described above. Holders of Reserved Shares will be required to execute agreements with the Company providing for certain restrictions on transfer and for the Company's right of first refusal.

Non-competition, Nondisclosure and Developments Agreements:

Each officer, consultant and employee of the Company will enter into a nondisclosure and developments agreement in a form reasonably acceptable to the investors. Certain officers and key employees will enter into non-competition agreements in a form reasonably acceptable to the Investors.

The Purchase Agreement:

The purchase of the Series E Preferred will be made pursuant to a Series E Preferred Stock Purchase Agreement drafted by counsel to the Company. Such agreement shall contain, among other things, appropriate representations and warranties of the Company, covenants of the Company reflecting the provisions set forth herein, and other typical conditions including (i) granting the investors reasonable access to Company officers and employees for the purpose of reviewing the Company's operations, and (ii) the obligation of the Company to acquire and maintain appropriate directors and officers insurance. The Purchase Agreement shall contain appropriate conditions of closing, including, among other things, qualification of the shares under applicable Blue

Sky laws, the filing of a certificate of amendment to the Company's charter to authorize the Series E Preferred, and an opinion of counsel.

Closings; Management:
There may be two or more closings provided that the initial closing must be in an amount not less than $3.5 million. By the time of the initial closing of the sale of the Series E Preferred, the Company will with the approval of the Board of Directors as well as a majority of the prospective purchasers of the Series E Preferred agree in writing to a general profile and line of reporting for a Chief Executive Officer as well as to the roles and responsibilities for the Founding members of the organization. The Board of Directors will commit by vote of the Board prior to the initial closing to initiate a search for a CEO subsequent to the closing and, on a best efforts basis, to work toward the hire of a CEO within the first 6 months of the initial closing.

Finders:
The Company and the investors will each indemnify the other for any finder's fees for which either is responsible.

Expenses:
The Company's counsel will bear responsibility for drafting of documents related to the transaction. The Company and the Investors will each bear their own legal and other expenses with respect to the transaction; provided, however, that assuming the successful completion of the transaction, the Company will pay the reasonable legal fees and expenses of Investors Law Firm LLC, counsel to the Investors, who will work on a best efforts basis to keep these fees to approximately $30,000 or less.

The foregoing terms are not intended to be and do not constitute a legally binding obligation but rather are solely for the purpose of outlining the proposed terms pursuant to which a definitive agreement may ultimately be entered into. This is not a commitment on the part of the Company to accept, or of any Investor to make, an investment in the Company. This summary of terms is not an offer, or an agreement, and a legally binding obligation will only be made pursuant to definitive agreements to be negotiated and executed by the parties.

6

ALTERNATIVES TO EQUITY FINANCING: TYPES OF DEBT AND BRIDGE FINANCING

In This Chapter . . .

The number one takeaway from introductory business school finance courses is that debt is typically less expensive than equity. This is generally the case for established businesses that can comfortably service debt from cash flow and thereby access additional capital at a market rate without diluting equity holders. For companies that are not yet cash flow positive and are in early or expansion stages of growth, debt-like facilities or leverage can take on several forms, each of which will be explored in this chapter. Depending on its form and the attendant expectations of investors, debt can create a host of costs and obligations for entrepreneurs. For this reason, entrepreneurs need to assess the trade-offs involved in leveraging the capital structure of their company and the possible implications for equity holders.

The terms and obligations attendant to various forms of debt that are made available to growing private companies are as specialized as those related to equity. This chapter will explore the different types of debt or debt-like financing and the typical terms associated with them that entrepreneurs need to consider. This chapter will review the universe of issues surrounding leverage for growing, venture-backed businesses that are not yet cash flow positive and conclude with an analysis of a form of term sheet used by a venture firm to propose one of the more common forms of debt to companies – the convertible promissory note, or what is often called "bridge financing."

Strategic Sources of Capital:
Alternatives to Traditional Debt

Astute entrepreneurs are usually acutely aware of the strategic value of their offering to potential strategic partners or acquirers but may fear accepting debt or equity investment from a strategic partner because of the perception that such an alignment compromises their independence and objectivity in determining strategic direction. It is critical to remember that capital that is commercially or strategically motivated does not need to take the form of traditional debt.

Strategic sources of capital that stand to gain incremental sales by bundling or co-marketing a growing company's offering can advance funds against future purchases. Such an approach can be treated like an advance against royalties with a cap equal to the amount of the advance. Consider the strategic corporate investor who expects to generate $10 million in incremental profit in a subsequent year by incorporating the technology of a venture-backed company into the strategic player's offering. If the strategic party expects to have to pay $5 million to the venture-backed company for the units of technology it plans to bundle in its offering, the strategic investor may be willing to advance the venture-backed player some amount up to $5 million and to treat this as a pre-payment toward future purchases.

Consider a second example in which royalties are a distinct alternative to debt financing. A prospective distribution partner for a venture-backed company could well look to the venture-backed company as a source of a new form of product for its customer base. In anticipation of selling some quantity of inventory, the distribution partner could advance the venture-backed entity a sum of money equal to the commission the distribution partner might receive on that quantity of inventory.

In both of these examples, it would be unlikely that the venture-backed entity would receive such advances without giving up something to the strategic partner. In all likelihood, some form of exclusive relationship would be demanded by the strategic partner for a defined period of time that would either equal or span beyond the term during which payback of an advance would likely be met.

Debt and the Capital Structure:
The Pros and Cons of Using Leverage

We all use debt or leverage in various ways in the course of daily life. Credit cards and home mortgages are good examples. For the established company with solid or prospectively growing cash flows, debt is attractive from the perspective of equity holders simply because each incremental dollar of debt does not dilute the equity position of equity holders.

Consider one company that raises $10 million in equity at $1 per share and a second company that raises $5 million in equity at $1 per share and $5 million in debt. While each company would have $10 million at their disposal, each share of equity in the company that raised $10 million in equity would hold 50 percent less ownership than each share of equity in the company that raised only $5 million in equity. Assuming that the second company is able to meet its obligations to its debtors and grow as quickly as the first, the potential value for equity holders is much greater. In the sphere of more mature cash-flow positive companies, it is not surprising, therefore, that leveraged buyout funds have evolved to be an attractive investment vehicle for investors. When growing, unleveraged businesses throw off a healthy base of cash, the cash flow from such businesses can often support a new layer of debt in the company's capital structure and afford the company the opportunity to use this additional capital for purposes of expansion, acquisition, or re-purchase of equity.

Companies that are not yet cash flow positive cannot by definition service debt without either receiving further infusions of capital or becoming sufficiently cash flow positive within a reasonable period after taking on debt so as to be able to meet debt obligations. While certain corporate cultures abhor considering any form of debt, most growing companies clearly aspire to generate the type of cash flows that would allow them to qualify for the types of credit usually afforded established firms. For established companies able to comfortably service debt, debt is often less expensive than equity because it does not dilute equity. Its one requirement is that it assume a higher place in the capital structure and less risk than equity. In liquidation, debt holders typically expect to be paid off first.

Venture-backed companies therefore are more inclined first to raise equity and, when they choose to use leverage of some sort, careful to balance the interests of equity holders with the risks and obligations associated with most forms of debt. Leverage is quite simply a sensitive and critical strategic issue for early-stage companies and their equity holders. While minority common stockholders usually hold little power to resist a company's decision to take on leverage of one form or another, leverage in any form of note challenges the typical powers of preferred stockholders. Preferred stock, while not senior to debt, is normally senior to common stock – and normally not quite so patient. Preferred stockholders may, for example, require that a company buy them out over five to seven years from a date of financing. This technically puts a term on preferred stock much in the way a note may. Preferred equity holders in effect usually hold a right to act like a bank and to require through negotiation a restructuring or liquidation if they have not received a return of capital within prescribed parameters and within a prescribed timeframe. Given this set of expectations, it is also quite standard that preferred stockholders also require their consent before a company assumes certain forms of debt.

Sources of Leverage

It is not surprising that the interest banks charge their established commercial clients is significantly below the rates of return required by note holders and other sources of leverage that the growing company may consider accessing. While equity is expensive enough – growing companies expect to give up a significant percentage of equity to angel and venture investors – debt in its various forms compromises a growing company's capital structure and often its strategic direction to various degrees.

Leverage for growing companies takes on two forms: those that are roughly aligned with equity holders and those that challenge the position of equity holders. Some forms of leverage do not significantly compromise the position of equity holders and are considered to provide an acceptable degree of leverage to a company or are embraced as strategically important. Others squarely compromise the position of equity holders in a company's capital structure and are mandated for important strategic reasons or because investors are simply not willing to invest in a form of equity and require seniority over equity holders.

Four common forms of leverage are available to early-stage companies – vendor financing, receivables financing, bank financing secured by individual personal guarantees, and bridge financing. The extent to which this range of options is limited is not altogether surprising, given the lack of cash flow typical to early-stage companies. Because early- and expansion-stage companies are not cash flow positive and therefore do not have a source of cash flow to service or pay off debt, the three types of leverage available to these types of companies usually come at a cost well above the standard financing terms that commercial banks would offer a cash flow positive, going concern. Usury laws prevent plain vanilla forms of financing available to venture-backed companies from being egregiously expensive. Interest rates typically cannot by law exceed 18 percent or so.

Of the four types of financing cited, the least expensive forms are vendor financing and receivables financing. While it may be possible to receive a third type of financing, bank financing, by convincing a bank to accept the guarantee of a wealthy individual, the individual or individual involved will likely require some form of warrant coverage or stock, making the effective rate of borrowing significantly more expensive than traditional bank debt financing or vendor or receivables financing. The most expensive form of debt available to early- and expansion-stage companies is that made available to them by a syndicate of venture or angel investors or by a specialist firm that provides bridge financing to venture-backed companies.

Vendor financing is the form of leverage that in many ways is the least onerous form to which an early-stage company can turn.

Vendor financing is secured against hard assets – computers and office equipment – and comes at the lowest cost to a company. Entrepreneurs who are trying to raise capital and point to a low level of capital expenditure from proceeds of a financing are best advised to consider leverage vendor financing as much as is practicable.

Receivables financing is often available from banks or specialized venture firms to companies with uneven or lumpy revenues and a strong client list whose payment stream is predictable but often extended. The extent to which a "factor" will need to assume some percentage of bad debt among a company's receivables will often influence adversely the cash flows that the company factoring its receivables can expect to receive. Between the percentage rate at which factors lend against receivables and the factors' assumptions about bad debts, a company can expect to sacrifice a significant portion of its receivables to generate consistent cash flow. When compared to the downside of a syndicated financing from venture investors with IRRs of 30 percent or greater, receivables financing nevertheless remains an attractive option.

A third form of leverage is sometimes available to young companies in the form of a line of credit or bank loan guaranteed by an individual or group of individuals. My discussion with Andrew McKee in Chapter Nine highlights how this form of financing can work with considerable success. In essence, a company that is considered an otherwise unattractive risk to a bank may be able to secure a line of credit or loan if that facility is guaranteed by a wealthy individual or group of individuals who pledge to make good on the facility should the company fail to be able to do so. Individuals would probably consider guaranteeing this form of leverage only if a company was willing to provide them with some upside to compensate for the risk involved in doing so. Upside could be granted in the form of warrants, for example.

The fourth form of leverage – bridge financing – serves as the main focus of this chapter and of the term sheet with which the chapter concludes. Bridge financing is typically sourced either from an existing syndicate of investors or a venture firm that specializes in providing bridge financing to venture-backed companies. Bridge financing is usually necessary because a company has run out of money from its last round of financing, but either expects to close on a new round of financing in the very near term or is unable to generate the confidence of its existing investors necessary for them to continue to invest in the form of equity.

Bridge financing is offered in the form of notes usually intended to tide a company over until a subsequent round of equity financing occurs, when the notes will either need to be repaid or convert into the new round of financing. Arguably, bridge financing can be considered a positive or a negative from the perspective of equity holders; certainly, it is risky, because it assumes a company can complete another financing by a certain date. A company that has generated significant momentum and is working toward a new round of financing at an improved valuation over previous rounds will typically consider bridge financing an important step toward a new round of financing and in the best interests of all stakeholders. Bridge notes in this scenario represent the commitment of existing investors to invest side-by-side with new investors in a new round of financing.

When an anticipated financing does not transpire, and new investors are apparently unwilling to consummate a financing, the implications of bridge financing and the terms of promissory notes challenge the position of equity holders. When a company requires bridge financing to continue to serve its financing needs, and the company is otherwise unlikely to attract additional capital from sources outside its existing syndicate of investors, the interests of note holders and equity holders tend to diverge. Note holders have the upper hand.

The extent to which bridge financing is expensive is entirely subjective. For the company whose prospects are rosy and which is likely to secure a new round of equity financing in the near term, nominal interest of 8 percent and, if necessary, a discount of 5 percent to 15 percent on conversion into the new round of financing may be adequate to provide the necessary sweetener a venture investor may look for. In such cases, the venture investor or syndicate of investors has full confidence in the likelihood of a financing at pricing the firm or syndicate of firms is likely to support.

If a company has failed to meet its operating goals and has consistently met with rejection in the capital markets, its group of existing investors may be its only source of capital for an indefinite period of time. Under these circumstances, existing equity investors who have available capital and a willingness to support the company are likely to demand a premium of return and seniority over prior rounds of financing and all existing investors. Such a premium will vary depending on the risk profile of the company and the perspective of the venture investors. Expensive terms are often associated with greed in the eyes of entrepreneurs and prudence in the eyes of experienced venture investors. Terms may include a discount of anywhere from 25 percent to 50 percent on the terms of the most recent round of financing, interest of 8 percent on the note, and security in the form of the assets of the company.

To encourage the possibility of a future financing, presumably including new outside investors, such bridge financing will be consummated in the form of a "convertible promissory note" – a note that also includes a feature giving the note holders the option of converting the value of the notes into a new round of financing. To ensure that note holders are "on the same page," it is not unusual for this conversion feature to require some majority of the note holders to convert together. The purpose of such a feature is to ensure that new investors are not put off by debt that is senior to equity on the balance sheet.

Term Sheet for Convertible Promissory Notes

The following term sheet is an example of a form used by venture investors to propose a syndicated round of convertible promissory notes for a company. In each section of the term sheet, an explanation appears in *italics* detailing the purpose and rationale behind the language in that section.

Case Study:
Company, Inc.

Summary of Terms for
Convertible Promissory Notes

Issuer:	Company, Inc. ("Company").
Investors:	Venture Firm One or affiliates, Venture Firm Two or affiliates and others (the "Investors")

Author's note: Most forms of term sheets include the names of the "lead" investor(s) as well as reference to "others," thereby leaving open the opportunity to other investors to participate. The term "affiliates" is included to accommodate the various funds that are associated with a firm and that may invest together the total amount a firm commits to a financing.

Type of Security:

Convertible Promissory Notes ("Notes").

Author's note: Convertible promissory notes are notes that serve as debt but convert under the terms of the financing. Notes can convert to equity automatically upon a certain event or at the discretion and choice of the note holder, terms that will be stipulated in the "Conversion Rights" section of the term sheet.

Closing:

It is anticipated that the Closing will occur on or about [Month] __, 2002, or as soon as possible thereafter.

Security:

The Notes will be a secured senior obligation of the Company, secured by all assets (including intellectual property) of the Company.

Author's note: Notes are not always secured, but when secured can be secured broadly, as in this case, or by specific assets of the company. Should secured notes come due and the company be unable to pay them or renegotiate payment terms, note holders take ownership of the assets of the company.

Terms of Notes:

Principal Amount of Notes:

Up to $500,000, to be advanced from time to time as needed, to be determined by the holders of a majority in interest of the Notes following a request by the Company.

Author's note: Principal can be paid in at one time at one closing or in multiple closings. The mechanics of a financing can allow that commitments can be received for one amount, and then multiple draw-downs of capital "called" as the company requires them. While this approach is clearly more complicated than one single closing, it can provide the company with more flexibility, should the company anticipate other sources of liquidity – a large pending contract, for example – that could satisfy the company's capital needs and prevent it from having to draw any additional capital.

Term of Notes: The Notes shall be due and payable on [Month]__, 2002, subject to extension by the holders of a majority of principal amount of the Notes to [Month]__, 2003.

Author's note: Extensions set expectations both for note holders who, in purchasing a minority of notes will need to follow the lead of the majority in a decision whether to extend or to "call" notes, and for the company.

Rate of Interest: Eight percent (8%) per annum, payable at maturity.

Author's note: Whereas "Prime Plus 1%" is not uncommon as a standard for notes of this nature, it is less likely to be adhered to when Prime is below 8%.

Conversion Rights: Notes plus accrued interest to the date of conversion may be converted by an Investor at any time into Series ___ Units of the Company at a 15% discount or may, at the Investor's option, convert into shares of the Company's securities issued in the next round of financing that is greater than $1,000,000 (excluding the Notes) (the "Next Round Financing") subject to the terms and conditions of the Next Round Financing; provided, however, if holders of a majority in interest of the Notes convert their Notes, all Notes shall automatically convert at such time on the same terms and conditions as the Notes of the holders of a majority in interest of the Notes.

Author's note: The rate at which notes may convert into a subsequent round of financing will vary depending on the risk associated with the bridge financing. In this round, the notes are discounted by

15%.

Prepayment:

The Notes may be prepaid in their entirety, at any time, without premium or penalty.

Author's note: The pre-payment clause gives the company the right to pay down the notes, providing it with the ability to relieve itself of the note obligation.

Use of Proceeds:

The proceeds from the sale of the Notes will be used for general corporate matters.

Options:

_____ additional options shall be created and granted at the discretion of the board to employees

Author's note: Every financing is dilutive to existing shareholders. Because the terms as outlined under the "Conversion Rights" clause typically result in additional dilution, the note holders may propose issuance of additional options to "protect" certain members of management from dilution. Whereas the dilution associated with bridge financing may "penalize" a company that has failed to perform, additional options may be appropriate particularly for those members of management who may not be directly responsible for the company missing its targets and who would otherwise be demoralized by the dilution.

Pro Rata:

Each holder of Series ___ Preferred shall be entitled to purchase Notes in an amount necessary for such holder to maintain his/its percentage ownership of Series ___ Preferred (on a fully diluted basis).

Author's note: It is typical that existing preferred stockholders be offered the right to invest in proposed notes for several reasons. First, when other sources of capital are scarce, their capital is attractive. Second, the terms of a bridge financing may be significantly attractive enough to create a conflict between the note holders and the provisions of the preferred, should each member of the preferred be prevented from participating. Third, even when members of the Preferred may be unable to participate, the offering protects those who do participate from future legal action.

Existing Notes:
All promissory notes issued by the Company for funds advanced to the Company previously shall be amended to provide that the terms of such notes will be the same as the Notes and shall provide for conversion in accordance with their terms in the event of conversion by the holders of a majority principal amount of notes of like tenor.

Author's note: The senior class of notes which are to be created further to the terms of this term sheet will want to be certain that any existing notes follow the lead of a new class of notes. This is stipulated so that in the event of a future financing or conversion mandated by an event considered in the best interest of new note holders, the old note holders do not serve as an obstacle to such action.

The Purchase Agreement:
The purchase of the Notes will be made pursuant to a Note Purchase Agreement drafted by counsel to the Investors. Such agreement shall contain, among other things, appropriate representations and warranties of the Company, covenants of the Company reflecting the provisions set forth herein and other typical covenants, and appropriate conditions of closing. Until the Purchase Agreement is signed by both the Company and the Investors, there will not exist any binding obligation on the part of either party to consummate the transaction. This Summary of Terms does not constitute a contractual commitment of the Company or the Investors or an obligation of either party to negotiate with the other.

Expenses:
The Company and the Investors shall each bear their own legal and other expenses with respect to the transaction, provided that if a sale of the Notes occurs, the Company shall pay the reasonable fees and expenses of one counsel to the Investors.

7

DUE DILIGENCE: HOW INVESTORS SIZE UP A COMPANY

In This Chapter . . .

"Subject to due diligence ..." This one central disclaimer is integral to the assumptions and discussion of terms with a VC and continues to prevail from the time the entrepreneur and VC agree to a term sheet until the closing of a financing. While a term sheet may bind the entrepreneur to a "no-shop" clause – to restrict the entrepreneur from "shopping" a term sheet and pursuing other sources of financing – a deal is not concluded until all of the VC's due diligence is completed, closing documents are executed, and cash is in the bank. For this reason it is critical for the entrepreneur to recognize that there are typically in reality two periods to the due diligence process – the period before the investor negotiates and agrees to a term sheet and the period between the time the term sheet is agreed to and the time of the closing of a financing. It is important to keep in mind that no one investor will follow the same due diligence process. In fact, some of the basic due diligence issues that some investors would typically examine before agreeing to a term sheet are not researched or reviewed by others until after a term sheet has been agreed to.

From the entrepreneur's perspective, it is only logical to assume that once a term sheet is agreed to, an investor has fundamentally decided to invest in the business as represented by the company. In reality, there is a host of due diligence issues an investor will need to explore before being comfortable enough to close on a financing. A company seeking financing should work to reduce or remove any significant risk that the investor might commit to a term sheet before becoming aware of information that might cause him to reconsider his investment decision or revisit terms. This is not to advocate that companies seeking financing obfuscate or distort their true state of affairs, but rather that they work to make sure they are proactive rather than reactive during the due diligence process.

A company seeking financing can be reasonably comfortable that an investor has undergone sufficient due diligence to be committed to a term sheet if the investor has, before the term sheet stage, been provided and engaged in reviewing the class of information that might be considered standard due diligence materials. These basics are reviewed in detail in this chapter to provide insight into the level of detail that such basic due diligence should require. An additional checklist of corporate records and agreements, while not discussed in detail in this chapter, is provided as an appendix entitled "Documents Likely to be Requested During Due Diligence." It is my view that this body of material, while often requested by an investor before the term sheet phase, is often not completely formally reviewed until well into the period between an agreement to a term sheet and the closing.

Certainly, it is always difficult to establish whether a prospective investor has truly absorbed the material with which he has been presented. Nevertheless, by being proactive and providing investors in advance of a term sheet discussion much of the information that is discussed in this chapter and detailed in the appendix, entrepreneurs can both minimize the amount of information a company will be likely to need to provide the investor after agreeing to a term sheet and hopefully know the investor is well informed about the opportunity in which he is committing to invest. Rest assured that experienced investors will do what it takes to make sure they have an intimate understanding of the asset they are backing and of what it will take for a company to execute its business plan before the closing of a financing.

How to Prepare

Anticipating the process a VC is likely to pursue during due diligence and the issues and documents likely to come under review will ensure a more predictable and quicker road to a closing. Some companies prepare binders of information in advance of initial on-site meetings with VCs, well before the term sheet process, in the hope of accelerating the VC's preliminary due diligence. There is, of course, a fine balance between too much and too little. Presenting a prospective investor with multiple books of photocopied and tabbed information before he or she has determined the interest level is overkill. Instead, it is more appropriate to understand and differentiate between the two distinctly different types of information an investor will look for during these two phases of due diligence.

This information can generally be grouped into two categories: information necessary for understanding the business and information in the form of documents, regulations, and agreements related to a company's corporate history, business practices, and operating environment. To the extent possible, it is important to ensure that both sets of information are readily available from the time the entrepreneur and the investor first engage and explore a potential financial partnership. While each investor may have idiosyncrasies or processes unique to their organization, information related to understanding the business will usually need to be absorbed before an internal preliminary investment decision by the investor's organization and a term sheet negotiation can proceed. It is entirely possible to weave a summary of almost all of this information into a business plan and other handouts or presentations.

The second set of information – the host of documents and agreements associated with a company's corporate governance and assets – is likely to be given only preliminary attention during the first phase of due diligence but more careful and detailed review during the second period of due diligence. This type of information is detailed in the appendix that outlines the type of documents VCs are likely to request.

In a very competitive marketplace, some VCs may go as far as submitting a term sheet to a company without fully researching or becoming familiar with the prospective investment and giving both groups of information only cursory review. Once the entrepreneur has signed the term sheet, and perhaps even agreed to a "no-shop" clause, the VC may in due diligence come to the conclusion that the investment is grossly over-valued, or the proposed investment structure needs to be renegotiated. This approach clearly sets up the entrepreneur for some surprises and potentially creates a level of mistrust that may result in a strain in the relationship that is difficult to mend. Therefore, I recommend that the entrepreneur ensure the VC has a good understanding of the company's business before proceeding to a term sheet. While getting a term sheet from a VC may be the entrepreneur's primary goal, the extent to which a business review by the VC has really transpired will ultimately determine the VC's assumptions and conclusions about an investment.

Peeling the Onion: Understanding the Business

To properly understand a business, the sophisticated investor will want to conduct an appropriate review of the business, management, research and new product development, marketing and sales, competition, financials, and prospects for an exit, any relevant production processes and facilities, public relations, and outsourced and service relationships. This is quite a shopping list of items a VC or sophisticated investor is likely to want to explore to fully understand a prospective investment. And there is a fine line between providing too much information and providing too little.

On one hand, the entrepreneur and the VC want to keep discussions focused. The entrepreneur ideally wants to provide just enough to whet the appetite of the prospective investor and to provide more as the investor asks for it. Providing too much may be a turn-off or may distract the investor from focusing on his primary area of interest. Providing too little may entice the investor to come to premature conclusions, deciding either to opt out of the opportunity or to tender a term sheet without fully understanding the opportunity, its upside and downside. I argue that both outcomes are negatives for a company. The offer of a term sheet based on inappropriate assumptions is likely to result in a renegotiation, due diligence that is full of surprises for both parties, and ultimately a changed and potentially irreconcilable set of differences. The risk of such an outcome will cost both the company and the VC a great deal of time, money, and lost opportunity.

There are ways to incorporate much of the information an astute investor is likely to need to see into a business plan and to provide additional information that is otherwise not appropriate for a business plan through other media, including handouts, articles, white papers, and presentations. While some of the minutia or detail related to topics and items in this general category are likely to bore or obfuscate discussions during initial meetings, it is important that the VC has access to enough information to understand the business before a term sheet discussion and agreement to terms can be concluded.

Here is an outline of the information a sophisticated investor will be looking for to fully understand a business.

Assessment of Business Mechanics

Investors will initially want to review five aspects of a business: organizational structure; markets and market positioning; products, suppliers, and external relationships; strategic plans; and product research and development and services.

Organizational Structure

"The jockey, not the horse..." Human capital and management expertise are the primary asset most venture capitalists want to evaluate when they examine organizational structure. In my opinion there are four core elements that provide understanding of a company's organizational structure.

1. An organizational chart and breakdown of headcounts by function or business unit clarify operating structure for the outsider. The investor wants to assess the execution capabilities and alignment of human resources within an organization.

2. Board structure and composition speak volumes about corporate governance, control of the organization, and the role of management on the board. VCs have a fiduciary responsibility to their investors to optimize returns on investments in companies. Ensuring that control and influence exist over the course of the growth and

development of an organization is central to the VC investment decision-making process.

3. A company's ownership history is likely to come under scrutiny. While it sometimes does not apply, if control or ownership has changed over time, the history, the outcomes of these transitions, and the extent to which the organization is encumbered by this history will influence a VC's opinion on whether there is potential liability that could become an issue in the future.

4. If a business is involved in the production or manufacturing of a product, a schematic layout of any facilities involved is appropriate.

Markets and Market Positioning

"Size of the market – is it growing?..." After "the jockey, not the horse...," these are typically the next words to roll from the lips of investors when asked what they will focus on in due diligence. Any good business plan will feature a section that sizes and qualifies the market in which a business is operating.

VCs tap five primary sources to verify market size and growth potential and to quantify the assumptions a company makes in predicting how much of that market they need to acquire to succeed. Company-provided information and references are one source, but clearly, unless these sources are independent, they are subject to the greatest scrutiny. Companies can, for example, work with advisors, academics, and industry experts who may develop a white paper or other information that serves to quantify market size.

An investor's personal network of industry-specific relationships is probably his or her other first source of due diligence. An established VC with, for example, semiconductor industry operating experience will make it his business to maintain as much knowledge as he can about every established player in the semiconductor space. Firms whose principals have strong operating expertise complementary to the market a company is pursuing will be able to quickly tap relationships with existing and successful market leaders. This has two benefits for them – information about current market dynamics and whether established players intend to play in a space, and information about the appetite for established players to acquire younger companies like those in the VC's investment sphere.

A VC's network of portfolio company and venture capitalist relationships is a second and equally fruitful source of market and due diligence information. The extent to which one can anticipate the strength of this network is often difficult for people outside a venture firm to gauge; the firm's advisors, venture experts, and principals' profiles, as well as the firm's list of portfolio companies, should be helpful.

In addition, venture investors typically subscribe to such services as CapitalIQ or VentureOne to glean information about private, venture-backed companies. These databases provide not only collected information about private company financings, but also information about board membership, management, and company focus. While these databases are typically not available to entrepreneurs, they reveal the extent to which investors' relationships are intertwined across industries and companies and the very powerful potential that exists for sourcing information through this network.

Alternatives to these networking approaches include information from and relationships at the independent market research firms such as AMR, Forrester, and Gartner, which produce sector- and company-specific information; however, this information is typically available only by subscription. Companies considered sector leaders should engage these organizations and work to position themselves as recognized leaders in sectors where the analysts of these research firms find vibrant market opportunities. If companies have access to these firms' relevant reports, they should pass them on to the VCs.

The fifth source of information for VCs with strong investment banking relationships is the sector- and market-related research produced by the research arms of these banks; but certainly the quality and motivations for investment banks creating this information have been scrutinized in the past. The extent to which this research is produced by the buy-side or sell-side of an organization will determine its independence, with buy-side information being generally more objective. You can bet investors who may not be entirely familiar with the market they are pursuing are highly likely to want to find ways of verifying that the business they are considering funding is both pursuing a sizable market and unlikely to need to penetrate a significant percentage of that market to succeed. The analysts at investment banks are tapped into the universe of market makers and, when interested, can be a sounding board for market trends and appetite.

The core set of questions prospective investors will ask regarding markets and market positions includes who principal competitors are and their estimated market share; comparisons to competitors based on price, margins, technology, and functionality; and strengths and weaknesses. A summary of any strategic relationships and partnering agreements or joint marketing agreements will need to be assessed and verified, and a list of top existing and prospective customers will need to be analyzed. Generally, VCs like to see that a company can penetrate 5 percent or less of a market but still be able to generate $100 million of market share in a market that is $2 billion (a size most VCs like). The market must be big enough to generate sufficient interest from VCs; 5 percent of a small niche is much less interesting, and claims that a company can achieve a large chunk or market share in a small market are often suspect. Therefore, it is less likely that a new entrant who needs 10 percent to 30 percent market share to generate $50 million or more in revenues will be able to prove they have a competitive and achievable business plan.

Products, Suppliers, and External Relationships

Companies fail when they execute poorly. Investors need to understand clearly the core competencies of the asset in which they are investing. It is critical to ensure that a company clearly and accurately represents its products or offerings and substantiates how the resources of the organization are leveraged to develop and market them. All too often, offerings are cluttered, poorly articulated, and differentiated or not well aligned within an organization. The age-old imperative to "focus, focus, focus" certainly applies. Companies that succeed provide core solutions to address specific problems and can point to customers who have quickly adopted these solutions as representative of a much larger universe of similar potential clients. It is very difficult to deliver a number of varied solutions or offerings to clients in multiple verticals simultaneously, so the logic and planning behind a company's product strategy will come under close and careful scrutiny.

Similarly, a company's relationship to and dependency on suppliers will come into question and review during due diligence. An investor needs to feel comfortable with the nature and relationship of suppliers whose solution is integrated into or part of a company's offering. The universe of suppliers that will come under scrutiny includes suppliers of production software, customer support systems software, and back-office software. Similarly, outsourced contract labor or services vendors whose solutions are bundled into an offering will come under scrutiny.

For each of these, it is important to be prepared to explain and verify the decisions and the rationale behind the selection of these suppliers. The most prudent approach for any organization to take is to keep summary binders and records that capture in detail all agreements with external entities, agreements related to facilities and real estate, service agreements, and intellectual property documentation and to indicate to investors where all of this can be reviewed.

Strategic Plan

Prospective investors will focus obsessively on what-if scenarios. Investors who understand the market a company is selling into will take great comfort in evidence of significant strategic thought and planning. The financials and business plan a company has prepared and presented to prospective investors will be considered a roadmap for the organization. It is not uncommon that such documents will be referenced in the documents closing a round of financing and, when agreed to by the company, used to benchmark or milestone a company's progress. Term sheets that propose milestones have contemplated these documents.

The checklist of issues investors will be looking to see have been addressed will include a near- to medium-term plan for technological research and development, a program to run management development and succession, and a strategy to continually assess and anticipate short- and long-term risks, volatility, and cycles.

Product Research and Development and Services

Some of the best investors, in my opinion, try not to get too excited by the technology and instead focus on evaluating other organizational assets. Indeed, in assessing an organization's product research and development strength, venture investors may well come to different conclusions, depending on the assumptions of the investor as to the role product research and development takes within an organization. It is critical, therefore, to understand the biases and assumptions of investors to communicate and explain the strengths of a product research and development organization.

Good investors are careful to take a balanced view of any company's technology. The technical assets of a company are indeed a source of that company's competitive advantage. However, sustainable competitive advantage is derived from a combination of a company's technical offering or solution and its ability to sell technical and service more successfully than competitors while continuing to improve technology to the extent that this is required to remain competitive and meet customer expectations.

Competitive advantage is, in my opinion, not necessarily derived from having a better technical solution. There are plenty of examples of companies whose success has been a function of a strong services organization, for example, or the look and feel of a particular interface, rather than enormously superior technology. My firm belief is that the best solution providers in the enterprise software arena, for example, are those who develop a strong services offering, or wrapper, as part of their technical solution.

An offering comprising both technical and services components typically requires a client to license technology and pay a recurring fee for services and maintenance. If a company's service offering is continuously integral to the client's ongoing use of an application or solution, a company can continue to work closely with a client and better understand both the client's evolving needs and how the company's solution should be adapted to suit clients over time.

Without a recurring revenue component and the discipline and incentive to continue to work with clients, a company's offering and solution can get stale, or the company can lose sight of how clients' needs change. If this happens, it would be only natural for the client either to look elsewhere for a better solution or, when looking at the original solution provider, to do so with some degree of dissatisfaction.

In assessing the product research and development assets of an organization, investors will first want to understand the context of product research and development as it relates to a company's offering and the history of product research and development within the organization. More specifically, the host of product research and development issues investors will look at during their initial business review will include assessments of product life cycle; project origination, planning, and controls; product acquisition opportunities; quality assurance and testing competencies and processes; technical service and support competencies and processes; and a comparison between the company's product research and development efforts and initiatives and those of competitors.

Sales and Marketing

The sales organization is a critical asset for any early-stage or growing company. Early-stage companies whose activities are most closely aligned with sales strategy are most likely to succeed. It is in this context that the best investors will evaluate all other activities within an organization – management, product development, and research, as well as a company's strategic direction and overall business plan.

As is therefore true for product development and research, alignment of organizational sales and marketing competencies with client acquisition is critical for an organization's success. The strongest investors will review sales and marketing activities to ascertain how their respective strategies are aligned and to understand the return on investment of activities in both of these areas.

Investors will typically look at sales initiatives and the sales organization as the primary revenue driver for an organization. Marketing activities are essentially evangelical until a strong list of reference-generous clients can be integrated into a company's marketing activities. When faced with the decision of marketing or sales spend, it is highly likely that committing resources to a sales force that contacts and acquires clients one by one is more effective than communicating resources to those marketing communication efforts that evangelize the merits of a solution, yet fail to point to a host of client experiences that substantiate the strength of an offering.

Sales and marketing due diligence, therefore, requires an assessment of the sales organization and an assessment of marketing programs. The hope and expectation of the prospective investor are that the two are well aligned. An assessment of sales requires an evaluation of both sales strategy and human capital. Sales strategy is all about execution; investors will want to see the universe of potential clients by size and geographic location profiled and clearly defined. A clear explanation of the sales process needs to be articulated and should include a breakdown of how each lead is qualified, how the sales process is assessed for success as the process progresses through a client organization, and how probabilities of closing are calculated. Investors will look closely at sales revenue plans and will look to see how predictably an assessment of the sales process and pipeline can point to expected revenues.

Sales Associate Profiles and Incentives

Sales associate profiles and incentives will also come under close scrutiny. Investors will check to see how sales professionals have been recruited and selected, how they are organized by geography, and how they are mentored and motivated. A company's selection process and bonus programs need to be well aligned with sales execution strategy. Sales professionals must be assessed based on their track record of delivering revenues at specific levels and for their sales methodology. A sales professional, for example, who has historically sold $2 million in revenues and received 5 percent in annual bonus on sales will need to see that he or she has equal or better potential within a new organization. If the sales cycle and model for a company's offerings are unlikely to allow that individual to generate similar economics or require a multiple of the individual's past performance for the company to meet revenue targets, the profile of sales professionals may be poorly aligned with the organization.

Similarly, the resources and support a sales organization requires to be effective will come under scrutiny. Growing companies depend on a certain degree of flexibility in how they prospect for clients and convert customers. Not surprisingly, one area in which investors are less likely to provide much flexibility at all is cost of customer acquisition.

Partnering Program and Distribution Channel Definition

A successful sales strategy should include partnering program and distribution channel definition and explanation. Investors want to see how the sales organization leverages external resources and partners because these entities can provide validation of and insight into the offering of a company. Nevertheless, partnering programs that create a layer of distance between a company and its client will come under close scrutiny. The predictability of a company's relationship with a client increases to the extent that a company is able to work directly with its clients, rather than depend on an intermediary to maintain an ongoing and profitable relationship. It is likely that partnering programs will come under heightened scrutiny if the revenues they are expected to generate represent a significant portion of overall revenues. The resources partners will contribute to a partnering program, the specific interest of the partnering entity in participating in such a program, and the motivation for a partner to succeed are all difficult to assess appropriately unless the investor takes the opportunity to speak directly with a representative from the partnering organization. Companies must therefore understand partnering organizations almost as well as their own and be prepared to represent the goals and objectives of the partnering organization with a level of familiarity that will convince investors of the likelihood of a partnership sales program succeeding.

Direct and Indirect Selling Strategies

The balance between direct and indirect selling must therefore be clearly defined, and the role of distribution partners explained. The balance and ratio of direct to indirect sales models is often a function of the scale and profile of a company's offering. If, for example, a company's revenue model generates very large licensing revenues and proportionately large recurring maintenance and service revenues, it is unlikely that a proportionately small ratio of direct to indirect selling would be appropriate. In this example, the prospective client would presumably decide to commit to a solution because of the client's confidence in the delivering organization, which could be harder to assess when working with a distribution partner during the sales process, as opposed to working with representatives of the company itself.

Pricing and Discounting Practices

Pricing and discounting are perhaps one element of due diligence review that can be most educational and revealing for investors. The pricing discussion will inevitably bring into question and review the economics of an entire company. Investors need to see the extent to which sales professionals understand the economics and profitability of the solution or offering they sell. Sales organizations and professionals who are given very lose reins and independence in cutting deals need to show a high level of competence and reliability in how they speak to pricing models and how they execute contracts. It is not surprising that some of the most effective private, growing companies have tight controls over the contract negotiation and pricing discussion process. Investors will want to see evidence that pricing economics and contract terms reflect a process of close communication among the sales organization, the finance organization, and parts of the organization responsible for execution.

Marketing Materials and Programs

In the same way that pricing models provide an informative and revealing snapshot of the economics of an entire organization, marketing materials and programs reveal the efficacy of an organization's strategy. Companies fail in execution; investors need to see that marketing programs and materials communicate a company's products and offerings with a voice and message aligned with a company's strategy.

Investors are likely to look very closely at return on investment when it comes to the marketing spend of a growing company. The productivity of each member of a sales team is relatively easy to measure; the value of each marketing dollar is incrementally more difficult to assess. So it is not unusual for investors to expect that marketing spend will represent a small percentage of overall sales and marketing spend. Small, growing companies, which have relatively little name or brand recognition, but which are intent on acquiring a relatively small percentage of an existing market are likely to be most successful by adopting a very targeted sales and marketing program. At such a stage of development, a company's advertising strategy will come under heightened scrutiny. Investors will want to see clear alignment of marketing spend with the revenue goals and sales strategy by distribution channel and offering.

Financial Structure

A company's financials come under significant scrutiny because they capture and reflect the essence of the historical and prospective profile for the organization and its business. Investors typically look for strong management teams and operating models that are highly predictable and reliable. So a company is most likely to execute predictably to the extent that a company's financials accurately reflect the assumptions and execution plans articulated by the organization.

One of the best ways for an investor to evaluate whether a company's profile is in any way significantly different from the way it has been represented by its core management team is for the investor to look for inconsistencies. Regardless of the discipline that is being evaluated, preliminary conversations with all stakeholders should, on balance, reflect a consistent message. A company's financials definitively capture information that should, on balance, be consistent with information derived from all stakeholders of an organization.

The four primary types of financial information an investor seeks to review are a company's cash flow statements, income statements, balance sheets, and audit reports.

Cash Flow Statements

Cash flow is very black and white. A company is burning cash, breaking even, or throwing off cash. Venture capital investors typically decide to invest in companies with the potential to build organizations that will ultimately generate revenues and cash flow that will command valuations at significant premiums over those at the time of investment.

Generally, the first order of business for venture capital investors is to see that a company can predictably grow to become cash flow positive with the capital a company's operating plan calls for. To do so, investors will look carefully at revenue and expense assumptions and work toward concluding whether cash flow expectations as represented by a company are, in the investor's opinion, an accurate prediction of the future. Looking retrospectively will produce one of the first clues to whether cash flow projections for the future are realistic.

In examining revenue assumptions, investors will come to an independent assessment about the size of the market a company is selling into, the pace at which a company is likely to be able to acquire customers, and the quality of the revenue associated with customers. Perhaps not surprisingly, an investor will look favorably on a company's revenue plan to the extent that the investor believes a company's revenue acquisition assumptions are realistic or conservative. On the expense side, the investor will look to see that the assumptions behind a company's execution plan as reflected in cash flow statements are consistent with the assumptions and statements made by the company's board and its management about the needs of its execution plan. Next, investors will consider whether these assumptions are realistic, ambitious, or conservative.

Income Statements

Investors are particularly sensitive to the quality, timing, and source of a company's earnings. So investors are likely to look closely at revenue recognition policies and accounting practices as determined by the company or by its board audit committee. Geographic distribution of revenue, as well as any trends among clients or economic factors, will also come under review. The trends of a company's own performance will be closely scrutinized as investors seek to decipher how margins have changed over time and how they may change with scale. So gross margins, operating margins, and net margins will all be considered from both a historical and a going-forward basis.

While net operating loss carry-forwards are of interest, they should not have a significant impact on an investor's decision to invest. They will nonetheless be of measurable interest.

Balance Sheets

The form a balance sheet takes is usually standard; however, given the sensitivity of cash and cash equivalents to understanding a company's cash flow and needs, the balance sheet will also come under scrutiny. Investors will need to review the balances of cash and cash equivalents at a company and assess the quality and nature of receivables. In reviewing receivables, a discussion of each of a company's clients and accounts will indicate for an investor the predictability of cash flow from key clients, particularly those who are a source of recurring revenue for a company. Investors will want to understand who manages receivables collections, what processes are adhered to, including receivables financing, and what the breakdown is of receivables by age – 30, 60, and 90 days, for example.

While not particularly significant in software or marketing companies, investors will want to review the actual hard assets of the company, including real estate, and approaches to amortization and depreciation.

The nature and size of long-term and short-term debt will be given particular scrutiny. For as yet unprofitable companies, equity investors typically do not look favorably on debt secured against the assets of the company. A company that is raising $5 million in new equity and expects to get to break-even on this amount of capital should expect investors to balk at six-figure debt on the balance sheet that is secured against the assets of the company.

Pro-forma Financials

Certainly historical financials will provide substantive evidence of an organization's ability to perform. But pro-forma financials are the blueprint to future success and in many ways reveal the extent to which a management team is capable of anticipating execution needs and challenges. VCs will dwell on forward-looking income statements, cash flow projections, balance sheets, and the universe of acquisition opportunities a prospective balance sheet could enable. The challenge for companies that are maverick or disruptive in a space is tying their prospective organizational model and cash flows to some reference point or financial model with which investors can identify.

Proven management experience and a track record of managing to plan in the past will be the greatest source of comfort for investors who analyze pro-forma statements. Padding numbers will only set in place a tit-for-tat between company and investor financial management. Conservative representations of future performance that can be tied to concrete revenue and execution examples are most credible in the eyes of investors.

Organizational Structure, Management, and Other Issues

Foremost in an investor's mind should be an assessment of organizational structure and management and how current and future plans for leveraging these aspects of the organization are aligned with financial models and sales and marketing objectives.

Physical Plant, Production, and Outsourcing

For organizations involved in production of product, an in-depth assessment of facilities, including an assessment of equipment and plant and attendant financial structures will come under review. Organizational and process design, as well as the trade-offs and benefits related to outsourcing, will come under review.

Other Significant Issues

Any patents, licenses, or trademarks in hand or in process of application are an important aspect of investment review. More important perhaps is disclosure of issues related to any legal proceedings, significant contractual relationships, or professional relationships. Relationships with other investors, as well as with attorneys, accounting firms, PR firms, and any other similar relationships or external validation in the form of news clippings, for example, can help better contextualize an investment for an investor. It is important to get these issues and relationships early in the engagement process.

8

THE LAWYER'S VIEW: INS AND OUTS OF SUCCESSFUL FINANCINGS

In This Chapter ...

This chapter features two interviews with legal experts in the private equity arena, one a private equity lawyer and the other general counsel to a leading private equity firm.

My earlier book, *Term Sheets & Valuations,* analyzes each of the terms that typically arise in a term sheet from three perspectives: company-favorable, neutral, and investor-favorable. To provide a no-nonsense perspective on what to look out for in a term sheet, the first part of this chapter features an interview with James M. Crane, who has served as counsel at the Boston law firm of Testa, Hurwitz & Thibeault, LLP, a seasoned lawyer who tells us what to look out for in a term sheet. Jim's perspective is representative of the candid, forthright demeanor that entrepreneurs and venture professionals look for in counsel.

The second part of this chapter examines the logistical coordination of the venture firms, legal teams, and company management from the perspective of Sarah Reed, General Counsel, Charles River Ventures.

What to Look Out for in A Term Sheet:
Discussion with Private Equity Lawyer James M. Crane

Alex Wilmerding: What exactly would you consider typical when looking for common ground in the form of a term sheet? Is there a neutral form of term sheet we can use as a starting or reference point for our discussion?

Jim Crane: While it is certainly relevant to include a balanced form of term sheet as a reference point, and I understand you have included one in the appendices of this book, it is frankly unlikely that any two lawyers would ever agree on the neutral form of any term. Each term sheet is affected by the subjective dealings of two parties; you can always come up with an argument for its favoring one party or another.

AW: Are the terms that are generally incorporated into a Series A Preferred by VCs created specifically for the current financing, or do they reflect some standard a lawyer or venture firm prefers?

JC: When you're talking about an early-stage preferred financing, a series A or perhaps a series B that occurs a year or two after the series A, very often the things that are coincidentally found in the term sheet and sometimes end up in the deal documents are terms that VCs have used in other recent financings.

AW: It may be most interesting for entrepreneurs to consider how lawyers look at a term sheet when representing a VC's interests. As companies progress through successive rounds of financing, it is standard that new VCs will bring new capital to a company. In these instances, it is important to consider how VCs interpret the terms presented to a company. Considering how VCs look at term sheets is important if entrepreneurs are looking for a perspective on the priorities VCs have when they draft a term sheet to be presented to a company. Let's consider the core terms to look out for in a term sheet. Which core terms do you first examine and consider when examining a term sheet that has been presented to you for review?

JC: The things that are important to me may be different if I'm representing a VC. A VC may draft a term sheet and have me review the draft before it is submitted to a company. A VC who is already invested in a company may pass me a term sheet that has been presented to the company by a prospective new investor.

If I am representing a VC who has a working first draft of a term sheet, the first thing I do is to take a quick look at the valuation of the company. The valuation section gives you a framework from which to work. The first questions I ask when examining valuation are the amount of capital going into the company and the price per share.

I also look closely at the key terms of the preferred stock. They may be a little different or have different protections, depending on whether it's a first round of preferred stock, a Series A round, or a later round, a Series E round, for example. If you're looking at a Series E round, very often just by way of precedent, the other rounds and their attendant leverage predetermine much of the nature of the framework and context for the terms of a Series E round. The extent to which the new money will have leverage over the old money will be spelled out here. A Series A, by being the first preferred to be issued, has the opportunity to define terms for the preferred. A Series E sometimes will need to incorporate provisions from prior classes of preferred that you have to live with. In these instances, you have to pick and choose your battles for things you want changed in the structure coming in.

In this respect, I always glance at the dividend provision, as well. I don't think whether there will be cumulative dividends is something a lawyer will dwell on, but the dividend provision is important to pay attention to, particularly when considering the implications for the preferred and the implications for a company with multiple classes of preferred, should they also hold dividend provisions.

Next, I look at vesting. What you'll usually want to do if you're the VC is to put right up front what you want the vesting of the founders' shares in an early-stage financing and the options pool to be. You don't want to create a situation where your founders can sneak out and leave the company high and dry when they are more often than not – and certainly in the early stages of the company's life span – vital to a successful venture. Beyond the economic parameters that some of the other terms mentioned will dictate, the restrictions on the founders and key employees will be critical to an early-stage venture's success. After a company has been around for a while, shares will have vested; and if the company is starting to make it, then maybe the importance of keeping any one individual starts to decline. Vesting schedules are probably the biggest thing to look at when I am looking at an early-stage term sheet. These schedules could be more important to consider than the terms for the preferred; if there are few restrictions in place on the founders' and key employees' stock, there is the potential need to issue incremental stock options.

While not considered part of the options pool, investors may also ask founders in an early-stage round to have their shares subject to vesting. This is sometimes generically referred to as "reverse vesting" – agreeing to have existing common stock, typically founders' shares, subject to vesting – to give founders incentive to perform. People don't often consider the importance of vesting schedules because people are trained to start digging into the terms of the preferred. And usually those provisions on the restrictions on the founder are stuck toward the back of the term sheet. But the implications for a company's future are significant.

AW: Options, and particularly the subject of vesting, are of great interest to entrepreneurs. Clearly, the terms defining vesting and valuation are, to some extent, interrelated. Is this a good example of the inherent flaw in dwelling too much on any one single term without considering implications of others?

JC: It is a good example of how many terms are intricately linked and cannot be considered entirely independently. The value you put on a company, assuming you'll add key people in the future, will be affected if additional shares need to be added to an option pool after a closing to provide appropriate incentive to management. I don't think this is necessarily obvious in the math of the valuation of the company unless, when you do your initial analysis, you consider vesting schedules for existing staff and whether the number of options included in the proposed capital structure at the time of closing anticipates options needs for the foreseeable future. For a relatively early-stage company, one that has been in existence for one or two years, language describing vesting schedules and treatment of options vesting should give a pretty good picture of the profile of a company's options pool.

Vesting and the subject of options are sensitive for founders because many have not been involved in this process before. With good reason, founders and key employees need to be prepared to accept the shock that their shares will be restricted right off the bat. Usually key employees and founders form the company. They set it up; they issue themselves common stock; and they think they own that stock. In a sense they do, but if they want to be financed, they'll have to put the restrictions on their ownership positions that the VCs are looking for, and that's often an emotional battle. I've had clients who were virtually throwing up at the thought that they had to turn over their shares and earn them back again. It is hard to educate highly educated people, but it is understandably new territory for them. Entrepreneurs can have trouble getting around it. The company's lawyers, if they have not done so already, have to get their clients to realize this is how venture financings work.

AW: Assuming entrepreneurs and companies are well advised, are there ways to anticipate some of this heartburn? What then are the preemptive strikes you would advise a company to make to mitigate terms that may appear on a term sheet?

JC: Accepting that a stock restriction agreement will be part of what will be expected by VCs is the first step. Very often what I do if I am representing a company in an early-stage investment is to try to preempt the VCs on this issue and set up the stock restriction agreement for the company and their founders before opening the negotiations with the VC. This way a company is prepared to say it already has an agreement in place, and it makes the issue a little tougher because the VCs then have to impose harsher vesting terms than the ones that already exist in the stock restriction agreement. If no agreement exists, it is easy for a venture firm to ask for certain thresholds straight off the bat. Many times, the VCs don't want to make enemies with the founders because doing so is in nobody's best interest, so changing an existing agreement may be something less likely to be initiated, once established.

You can't really preempt VCs on any of the charter provisions and preferred stock terms. Usually a new company will have a very plain vanilla common stock charter. The VCs typically will come in and know what they're looking for, and you may have to redo your whole charter if they want to make changes. Probably the only meaningful battle you can preempt the VCs on is the type of vesting. You have to take an educated guess based on where the market is in any particular month. A common VC approach is to have founders' shares put on a four-year vesting term. Entrepreneurs may try to preempt the vesting issue for their existing shares by adopting an agreement to have one-third vested immediately and the rest on a three-year term. Often the VCs will come in, and, depending on the relationships and how much they want to offend the parties, they'll say they'll let that stand. This is a good way for VCs to express their acknowledgement of the founders' value before the game even starts.

AW: Let's move on to liquidation preference, which is often a sticking point and an important term on which to focus. What do you look for when examining a liquidation preference clause?

JC: Liquidation preference is really what the deal is all about. The liquidation preference section defines how much each class of preferred stock will receive in preference to other stockholders if a company is sold or generates liquidity as a result of a transaction before any of the other stockholders receive proceeds. The definition of a liquidation event is therefore very important; it will define when liquidation preference terms take effect and how individual classes of preferred shareholders will be treated as compared to common. Liquidation will be defined as an actual dissolution of the company, and the definition could also include a merger, an acquisition, a sale of the company, or a change of control of anywhere from 50 percent to 80 percent to 100 percent of the voting power of the company – often referred to as a deemed liquidation. In the event of what is defined as a deemed liquidation of the company, liquidation preference terms would take effect.

AW: What other term sheet text may reveal preferential treatment to the preferred?

JC: If protective provisions are incorporated into a term sheet, the preferred are looking for a form of blocking power to block management from making certain decisions without their approval. Protective provisions typically require that a certain percentage of the preferred be required to vote to approve certain actions the company chooses to take. Without the vote and approval of a certain percentage of preferred stock, the company is blocked from taking certain actions. For example, protective provisions can stipulate limits on the amount of debt a company can take on.

AW: How might protective provisions restrict a company from increasing its option pool or pursuing a subsequent financing without prior approval?

JC: Protective provisions could restrict certain actions, including amending the charter of the company, pursuing a merger or acquisition, and increasing the size of the equity pool, for example.

On the subject of options, protective provisions that require approval of some majority of the preferred to make any amendment to the charter of the company in effect limit a company's ability to increase its options pool beyond the authorized shares stipulated in the charter. The charter will detail the total authorized capital stock of the company, which has a limiting effect on the number of shares in the company's option pool. If the company wanted to increase the option pool and protective provisions required that approval from some majority of the preferred be secured to do so, the company would in effect be restricted from increasing the options pool unless some majority of the preferred were to approve an amendment to the charter. Assuming a company has an options pool of sufficient size to serve its needs, this power will give the preferred a degree of leverage, should a board and management look to increase the size of the options pool at some future point. If, subsequent to a financing, additional options were required to create an additional incentive for additional staff, a further increase to the size of the options pool would be dilutive to the preferred. The preferred may exercise their blocking power to, in effect, require that the existing option pool be reapportioned, for example. Such a provision does not have to be an obstacle to future expansion to an option pool; companies that meet and exceed the business plans they commit to and that require an expanded option pool to accommodate growth will most probably receive the support of their investors if such an initiative is in line with investors' expectations.

Protective provisions may also forbid the issuance of additional stock and hence a subsequent equity financing without approval of some majority of the preferred. This is an additional source of leverage for the preferred and presumably a deterrent to management who might otherwise assume that serial rounds of equity financing could be a panacea to their capital needs.

AW: How creative can investors and lawyers get with protective provisions?

JC: You can incorporate just about anything your heart desires. There are certain terms you almost always see, such as in the case of a merger or sale of the company. Similarly, provisions preventing changes in the nature of the company's business are not uncommon; an investor does not want to be buying stock in a company that's doing X, and the next thing they know the company's doing Y instead.

AW: How are protective provisions of some early form of preferred – a series A, for example – incorporated into future rounds of preferred?

JC: One thing that's important for a late-stage company financing is for the interests and therefore the protective provisions associated with early rounds of preferred to be balanced with the interests of later-stage investors. A company does not want investors from early rounds who may not have the capital to participate in later rounds of financing to hold the power to prevent the company from pursuing a good deal later on in the life of the company. It would be very unlikely that a Series B would agree to let an
existing Series A vote independently on this issue unless, of course, the investors in the Series A and the Series B were the same. Instead, often a later series of preferred will require the protective provisions of earlier preferred be revised so that all classes of preferred vote collectively.

AW: We've talked about valuation, vesting, liquidation preference, and protective provisions. What's next on your list?

JC: One of the most important things is the impact of dilution protection provisions. That's always a key thing. In the term sheet stage, negotiating the terms for dilution protection provisions is not always easy. Often investors won't actually spell out the dilution protection provision formula in the term sheet; they'll wait to do so in the final definitive closing documents. They just say a weighted-average formula.

AW: But there are several types of weighted-average formulas.

JC: That can be the tricky part. It probably would be a better practice to actually put the formula into the term sheet, or at least clearly define it. It's not as much of an issue if anti-dilution is a full ratchet because that's pretty cut and dry. If it's a later-stage company, maybe it's not so much of an issue because they've had a weighted-average formula in their charter, and the VCs have already seen it, and they'll just go with it. In an early-stage company, there might be a little bit of an argument about which shares will be included in the anti-dilution formula when you actually get to the drafting stage and have to put the language in. At that stage, there may be disagreement over what shares are included in the calculation.

Another thing is that you'd be amazed at how often someone can later go back to the formula, or the language if there is no formula, and it doesn't read right. It's very tricky to use the English language to write out a mathematical formula. The language is awkward and weird, and it gets screwed up more often than you think it should. This is the nuts and bolts of the economics of the deal, and I think it's critical that any time you're going through anything involving numbers in a term sheet, you actually do the math and make sure the numbers work. I never read an anti-dilution provision and say, "Oh, that looks right. Those are the words I'm familiar with." Even if I am 99.999 percent sure that's the way I have seen them every other time, I still take out my calculator and a pen and paper. I take some numbers from the term sheet somewhere else and assume a scenario and plug in numbers to see how it comes out. Sometimes a very subtle mistake in how the words are transcribed from whatever previous deal you used will screw up a formula.

AW: Let's consider the IPO process and how it is reflected in term sheets. Could you comment on registration rights and how they are treated?

JC: Registration rights are almost more of a leverage tool that plays later on when a company goes public. This subject does not necessarily get a lot of attention from entrepreneurs when they are focused on getting enough capital in the door to get to cash flow break-even. Registration rights are one area of language in a term sheet that levels out the most in a down market – IPOs are more distant in everyone's minds.

The things to look for there are the number and types of registrations and the time frames involved – how quickly a registration can be forced and when the registration rights expire. Very often registration rights agreements will have some built-in expiration, usually based on a period of time or when the shares become otherwise salable, for instance under SEC Rule 144.

The expenses of registration are another thing to focus on. Typically the company bears the cost of registration, but if someone requests a registration and withdraws the request, it is not uncommon for the company to retain the right to pass the expense on to the investor who requested the registration. This is one important way for a company to put in place disciplines that encourage investors to make sure their requests for registration are well thought out. On the other hand, if you're a VC, you might agree to this approach but try to ensure that expenses will be covered by the company if the registration is withdrawn for reasons that were beyond the VC's knowledge or ability to foresee. A war or bombings that rattle the financial market are extreme examples.

Investors will also want to include piggyback registration rights; they will want the right to participate not only in the first but also in subsequent public offerings. Investors will want to detail what happens if there's a cutback in how much stock can be sold on the public markets; they'll want to detail how each type of stock will be treated. Usually there will be a hierarchy: If there's a cutback, this one goes first, and we'll take it from there. I've seen some cutback provisions that get quite intricate about who gets to register their shares in what order. But often that level of detail is worked out in the deal documents and not in the term sheet. "With appropriate cutback provisions" is about as specific as the term sheet language will get.

One thing that's very important with respect to registration rights is that you don't want to have a lot of registration rights agreements out there. It's important that everyone is all tied up in one agreement. It's easier and less complicated because you don't want to have to go back through the old terms. If there are varying terms you want, at least try to have them all in one document, so you have only one place to look to find out where everyone stands. You want to have everyone who has registration rights at all to be party to the one agreement.

Whether you're representing the company or the investor, I can't imagine a scenario where it would be in your interest to allow multiple registration rights agreements out there. The registration rights contained in the agreement are rarely used, but it's an extremely powerful tool that has very powerful consequences for everyone registering shares for public sale. You don't want those rights to just be floating out there – you want to know where they are, and you want everyone to be wrapped up in the same agreement. If you don't do that, or at least vigorously fight for it, then I don't think you're doing a service to anyone. Usually there's no objection at all – I've never had anyone say no to it.

AW: Give some examples of how term sheet style and approach can be unique.

JC: The terms commonly used by one investor for one type of deal can begin to creep into term sheets for companies facing very different situations for which such terms may not be appropriate. Take for example an investor who's been working in an environment where they go into struggling companies because they can pick leverage situations or turn companies around long enough to put some money in and then get out. It is not uncommon to see the terms used by these individuals popping up in term sheets in early-stage ventures where such terms may not be the common practice. Often when companies are struggling, the term sheets and deal documents might include milestones that spell out consequences for the company's failure to meet those milestones. Very often these consequences might include existing stockholders losing control of the board and investors taking control of the company if the company is not performing. In a different investing context, such as an early-stage financing, if you have a VC who's used to getting those terms, it's harder than you'd think to get them to drop them.

The most dangerous thing about term sheets is for an investor to get into the habit of just grabbing the last one he had from a recent deal and revising it. Whenever I'm asked, I'll provide an original term sheet that covers all the bases. Term sheets are restrictive in nature because you're stuck with the terms spelled out on the page. As the corporate attorney sometimes you'll be given a draft of the term sheet you'll recognize from having worked on it in a previous deal. Just because you did it last time doesn't mean you want to do it this time. I try to start with a blank term sheet, not one I've used before.

There's nothing wrong, however, with using a form as a tool, as long as you use it in the right way.

I have a formal term sheet I like to look at, but it doesn't have everything that could possibly be incorporated into a term sheet. This one has suggestions for alternatives, bracketed items, and notes about things to consider. It includes alternative clauses. It does not have everything. When you keep building off an older version of a term sheet, at some future point, you'll miss the chance to take another direction because the forms you always use say X, and you've forgotten the alternatives because they are not in front of you or you haven't had them in your deals lately. You've forgotten about the possibility of doing Y instead.

AW: Is there a strategy you recommend people follow when negotiating a term sheet?

JC: It depends on the facts for the particular deal and your sense of what's important to the company and to the VCs. As for the pricing and that kind of thing, that's better left out of the hands of the lawyers. Very often that's been settled before the lawyers even get the call from the client to look at the term sheet.

I don't know that I have any advice on strategy that would apply to every situation. I think in early-stage investing, the key is the founders and their level of sophistication. If they're not sophisticated, investors may end up having problems getting past the hurdles I mentioned before, like the vesting on the founder ownership, which is hugely important. I don't know if there's a good way to soften them up before an investor starts hitting them with the other points. It really just depends on the people involved and the facts of the situation.

AW: Have you seen really gross variances or differences in the evolution of the term sheet over the years?

JC: Over the past five years, the staples of term sheets have remained relatively the same, and yet we have seen a big swing from company-favorable to investor-favorable financing climates, influencing which party the language favors. Consider protective provisions, for example. In a company-favorable investment climate, it is almost unheard of for a company to have a charter with a ratchet provision or very onerous provisions. In a more investor-favorable climate, the deals happen at a slower pace, and there's more time to negotiate in favorable terms. When deals are happening so fast that it may seem there are other VCs around the corner, in some cases, tripping over themselves to give a company money, investors are unlikely to incorporate extensive protective provisions. In both types of investment climates, the issues are the same. The biggest shift is in the negotiating leverage. In a very company-favorable climate, there are a lot of vanilla terms, and deals get papered very quickly. As the deals slow down, the terms get negotiated harder, and companies find themselves with more terms they have to live with.

AW: Do larger law firms have certain views about how much work they'll do for early- or expansion-stage companies?

JC: Large firms will be selective; they often will not get involved in every angel round. That's not to say they won't do them if there's a relationship there or something they're interested in. Usually the angel rounds happen at very small amounts, and the terms aren't so complex; it's a friendlier negotiation, and everyone is just trying to get the company into the game. The company is not quite ready to venture into the real arena yet, so they don't need a large venture law firm to work on the documents. There are individuals or small firms that will do it, and there are groups of angels who support them. Either way, you want to engage a qualified professional, with experience, who won't create problems in documentation that will cost more money later to fix. Angel investors get in and pay attention to protecting their ability to stay in the game and going forward a little bit; they're trying to make sure that down the road they're not just lumped in with common. Such terms are not necessarily complex enough to justify use of a large firm.

AW: How would you recommend an entrepreneur go about selecting a lawyer or a particular firm to work with?

JC: In the very early stages of a company, you at least want someone who's done this before who can hold your hand. The point is that there's almost nothing in the term sheet that isn't worth looking at. Depending on a company's bargaining position, it's important for a company to get good legal advice because you never know to what extent great thought has been put into the term sheet that may be presented to you, or if it's a remake of a previous form – some terms might not be entirely germane to the company in negotiation.

Logistical Coordination of Venture Firms, Legal Teams, and Company Management:
Guidance from Sarah Reed, General Counsel, Charles River Ventures

Sarah Reed, general counsel to Charles River Ventures, which has offices in Waltham, Massachusetts, and Menlo Park, California, is a renowned speaker and mentor in the field of venture capital transactions. She has made available to us her "cookbooks" for successful first and follow-on financing transactions as well as provided insights into the rationale behind these "cookbooks" in the form of an interview. These frameworks provide an organizational plan for the teams of lawyers who represent entrepreneurs in a financing. You would do yourself a service by floating a copy of one of Sarah's cookbooks to your legal counsel.

These cookbooks and the dialogue that follows are featured here as concluding sets of information for entrepreneurs who are keen to respect some simple legal advice about coordinating the drafting process before a closing and the volumes of e-mails and paper that are passed among established venture firms, their legal teams, entrepreneurs, and the teams that represent the entrepreneurs.

While you should keep in mind that Sarah's cookbooks are intended for circulation to the legal counsel of companies receiving financing, the message of these documents and the dialogue is clear: Entrepreneurs, VCs, and counsel alike need to be aware of the ins and outs of managing the legal process up to a closing.

When I asked Sarah about her motivations for authoring her cookbook, she said:

> My motivation was pretty simple. The ministerial aspects of these transactions were highly cookie-cutter, but because there is almost always one new law firm on one side of the transaction that is not familiar with your firm's standard operating procedures, I was finding that on every deal, I was wasting cycles getting at least one party up to speed on our SOP. For example, on my first five deals, I found myself having to tell the parties that wiring instructions should be sent to our accounting department, not to me. It pretty quickly occurred to me that it would be much easier to prepare a cookbook outlining our SOPs, which I could then send out at the beginning of each deal, instead of having to send the same dozens of e-mails on every deal.

Cookbook for a Successful FIRST Financing Transaction with [Venture Capital Firm]

1. [Venture Capital Firm] Financing Working Group ([working group e-mail address]) (which in turn consists of [name and e-mail addresses of members of working group]) should be on distribution list from outset of transaction, copied on all e-mails.

2. Please send [working group] a working group list as early as possible.

3. Please do **not** copy the investing partner on e-mails that involve only technical legal and/or drafting issues.

4. Please do **not** copy the investing partner on all the iterations of the documents before the deal closes.

5. Please **do** copy the investing partner on all iterations of the disclosure schedule.

6. When circulating documents that have only a few changes *(e.g.,* the final revision of the document), please summarize any material changes in the text of the e-mail – or state that there are none.

7. Please provide [Venture Capital Firm] *timely* updates on the expected closing date – we need to know what the expectation is from the outset, and need to know when, and for whatever reason, the timetable has changed.

8. [Name and e-mail address] is the contact for signature pages. Please contact him/her early in the process to get the correct signature blocks. Please endeavor to get to him/her any signature pages you need executed by [Venture Capital Firm] one day before the deal is to close.

9. Please send wire instructions to [working group] at least one day before the deal is to close. **We must receive the instructions to wire before [wire deadline] p.m. Eastern time** in order to fund on that day. When everything is in order for closing, and the wire is ready to go, please inform [working group].

10. Please send us a closing binder as soon as one is available, Attention: [name and mailing address].

11. Please send the stock certificates as soon as they are available, Attention: [name and mailing address].

12. At or shortly after closing, e-mail to [name and e-mail address]:

   (a)   the attached (completed) deal summary sheet

   (b)   the final cap table

   (c)   the final deal documents

13. Below are some of the "[Venture Capital Firm] standard" provisions that we would like to see incorporated in the documents.

   Cap Table

   Please include a detailed cap table as an exhibit to the securities purchase agreement (referenced in the capitalization representation).

   Indemnification

   In the Charter (or bylaws, at minimum), we like to ensure that …

   Definition of _____

14. [Venture Capital Firm] always requires a management rights letter. Attached is our standard form.

Cookbook for a Successful FOLLOW-ON Financing Transaction with [Venture Capital Firm]

1. [Venture Capital Firm]'s Financing Working Group ([e-mail address for group]) (which in consists of [names with email addresses]) should be on distribution list from outset of transaction, copied on all e-mails.

2. Please send [working group] a working group list as early as possible.

3. Please do **not** copy the investing partner on e-mails that involve only technical legal and/or drafting issues.

4. Please do **not** copy the investing partner on all the iterations of the documents before the deal closes.

5. Please **do** copy the investing partner on all iterations of the disclosure schedule.

6. When circulating documents that have only a few changes (*e.g.,* the final revision of the document), please summarize any material changes in the text of the e-mail – or state that there are none.

7. Please provide [Venture Capital Firm] *timely* updates on the expected closing date – we need to know what the expectation is from the outset, and need to know when, and for whatever reason, the timetable has changed.

8. [Name (e-mail address)] is the contact for signature pages. Please contact him/her early in the process to get the correct signature blocks. Please endeavor to get to him/her any

signature pages you need executed by us one day before the deal is to close.

9. Please send wire instructions to [working group] at least one day before the deal is to close. **We must receive the instructions to wire before [wire deadline] p.m. Eastern time** in order to fund on that day. When everything is in order for closing, and the wire is ready to go, please inform [working group].

10. Send us the attached (completed) deal summary and the final cap table at the time of closing.

11. Please send us a closing binder as soon as one is available, Attention: [name and mailing address].

12. Please send the stock certificates as soon as they are available, Attention: [name and address].

13. We always require a management rights letter (unless one has already been obtained in the prior round). Attached is our standard form.

14. Please include a detailed cap table as an exhibit to the securities purchase agreement (referenced in the capitalization representation.

Featured here is the interview I conducted with Sarah Reed. Our discussion further explores the evolution of her "Cookbooks," as well as her perspective on the ins and outs of managing the venture financing documentation and closing process.

Alex Wilmerding: Entrepreneurs in particular need to have a clearer picture of the issues that counsel representing them should anticipate when dealing with counsel representing investors and VCs. Can you walk through the rationale of each of the points in your cookbook?

Sarah Reed: In terms of the ministerial aspects of the transactions, it is always handy to have a working group list that is the essence of the first two points in my two cookbooks. This should include all members of the accounting team, as well as the legal team, for both sides of the transaction. Without the benefit of a complete working group list, sometimes communication with partners at law firms can be drawn out. For venture firms that outsource legal work, the only people VCs are aware of often are the partners at law firms; the partners are not actually the ones doing the work, so it is pretty important to know who the guy is who is actually lifting the pen and commenting on the documents. Otherwise, I am wasting everyone's money and time if I call the partner, whose response will be "Great, I'll get back to you..." – after he consults with the associate who is actually doing the heavy lifting on the deal. That's why a working group list is so important.

Points 3 and 6 in the cookbook deal with minimizing excessive e-mail volume. When there is a minor change to a document – the closing date, for example – the VC partner in a large firm just does not need to see a completely new set of documents if there is in-house legal counsel or someone appointed to be point person other than the partner. The partner does need to be briefed as to the change, and this is the role of general counsel in a larger firm. I view myself as the buffer zone between lawyers and the partners: It is my job to inform the partners of any substantive and material changes in the documents – I will never clutter their inboxes with voluminous redlined documents they have to pore through themselves to determine whether there are any material changes.

AW: The use of certain terms can become standard operating practice for some venture firms, something that is difficult for entrepreneurs and their lawyers to fully appreciate. Please comment on the type of relationship that exists between venture investors and their lawyers.

SR: A huge conundrum of a lawyer's job is that they are not actually empowered to make any decisions on their own. They always need the client's input – but in many cases the VC does not want to be bothered with these issues. It is a sensible practice, therefore, for the lawyer with a VC client to ask the client for blanket marching orders on certain points. This is captured in points 3 and 4 of the cookbook.

AW: Talk about point 5, the disclosure schedule; 6, which details etiquette for circulating documents that have only a few changes; 7, which mandates the need for timeliness; and 8, which discusses signature blocks.

SR: The partner in a venture firm needs to see every version of a disclosure schedule; this is why point 5 is very important. The disclosure schedule contains business issues, and the venture partner responsible for the deal should not be surprised by anything they see on that schedule.

Point 6 exists to prevent those non-descript e-mails stating nothing more than, "Attached please find a black-lined version of these six documents." The e-mail should provide some introductory summary of the material changes so that the reader does not need to scroll through all six of the documents to find where the black-lined areas are and what they amount to.

Point 7 is important because venture firms have to budget when they need to make capital calls and need pretty good visibility as to what deals are coming up when. They are not necessarily just sitting on cash waiting for a closing, particularly if the date for a closing becomes a moving target.

As to point 8, we almost always send the signature pages in advance and have them held in escrow, particularly if there is a chance that the partner might not be available for signing at the necessary time.

AW: Points 9 through 12 are fairly self-explanatory. Talk about a few of the things that are not negotiable for venture firms and that are drivers for points 13 and 14 in your cookbooks.

SR: The actual substance of these "deal standard terms" will, of course, vary by firm, and even by partner within a firm. At our firm, for example, we like to have a detailed post-closing cap table attached to the Stock Purchase Agreement so that we can always have it available in the closing binder.

A management rights letter, referenced in point 14, is non-negotiable for venture capital firms that have any ERISA investors (pension plan money). ERISA investors are permitted to invest in venture capital as an asset class only as long as the venture capital firm in question qualifies as a "Venture Capital Operating Company (VCOC)" within the meaning of the relevant ERISA regulation. In essence, a VCOC is one that takes an active role in its investments. A management rights letter simply provides that the VC firm will have certain "active investor" rights in connection with its investment to be ERISA compliant.

AW: What would you advise an entrepreneur to look for in the law firm it hires?

SR: I would want to make sure the firm has experience in venture capital finance, either company side or VC side. I have found it really matters to have counsel who understand the basic ground rules. I did one deal where the entrepreneur's lawyer had never seen a venture term sheet and thought, for example, the concept of redemption rights was outrageous. He told his client that basically we were asking for an unconscionable term – even though redemption rights are absolutely plain vanilla. That deal was ultimately derailed because the entrepreneurs' lawyer scared his clients to death about the deal terms – which were in fact very entrepreneur-favorable by industry standards.

One of the important functions experienced counsel can provide an entrepreneur is understanding what is actually negotiable. A lot of venture capital investors are used to just setting their terms; most of these standard terms are often, from the firm's perspective, very fair. When you are doing really early-stage investing, 90 percent of what you are investing in is character and people. If an entrepreneur appears unreasonable about something that is fairly standard in the industry, the partner is likely to say, "Forget it; the deal is off." Good counsel will help an entrepreneur navigate terms that are fairly standard and understand what is and is not negotiable.

AW: How would you profile the differences in stages in financings and how terms change from an A round to a C round?

SR: It is so important to be thoughtful about the series A terms because you are setting the template here for later rounds. Some lawyers and VCs are too focused on short-term implications, without thinking through the ramifications for later rounds. For example, anti-dilution disproportionately benefits later-round investors who invest at higher prices, so you need to really think about putting it in the Series A, and you certainly don't want to include it unless you definitely plan on investing in later rounds.

AW: How do you generally think companies can prepare for due diligence so that it is a much less costly and time-consuming process?

SR: Pay attention to actually keeping files. If a company anticipates an upcoming financing, they should start organizing documents into binders and files (for example, material contracts, equity comp documents).

9

RAISING
CAPITAL

In This Chapter . . .

The core of this chapter is an interview I conducted with entrepreneur and private equity investor Andrew McKee. Andrew is founder of Vacation.com and is currently a general partner of Webster Capital, a Cambridge, Massachusetts, organization that syndicates financing for later-stage, consumer-oriented companies. In addition, he is an active member of a Massachusetts-based network of angel investors, the Hub Angels, which focuses on making investments in early-stage companies with great market opportunities and unique technology.

Those of us who witnessed the dot-com financing cycle associate many of the financings that transpired during that period with relatively free-flowing capital and high valuations. It is important to keep in mind that the first period of Vacation.com's growth began in 1994, before the dot-com financing boom. So the history and experience of entrepreneur Andrew McKee at Vacation.com span both the more rational economy of the early 1990s and the heady times of the late 1990s. His is a fascinating perspective on capital raising and the choices entrepreneurs face when pursuing equity and debt capital from friends and family, as well as capital from venture capital firms and strategic partners.

The second section of this chapter is a conversation with Ginny Davis Wilmerding on the merits of using third parties to manage the process of raising capital. She also discusses setting the terms of engagement for working with these placement agents.

Discussion with Andrew McKee, Entrepreneur and Private Equity Investor

Alex Wilmerding: As background, tell me about your role at Vacation.com and the financial history of the company.

Andrew McKee: I was the founder of Vacation.com, which was known at its inception as a marketer of vacation products to consumers through online services. The company was founded in 1994, when the Web was just in its infancy. I had founded two companies before Vacation.com, one in the tour business and the other in the music retailing business. I founded Vacation.com as an online marketing service for the leisure and vacation package industry, as opposed to the airline, hotel, and car distribution business, which was focused on subsequently by companies such as Preview Travel, Travelocity, and Expedia. My role as founder of Vacation.com was to bootstrap the company and, of course, I was always searching for investment partners. I founded the company as a business to consumer business (B2C), offering vacation products to consumers who would buy directly from us, as they would an online travel agency. We achieved reasonable volume and success, but felt the real opportunity was as a technology provider. So we evolved into a business to business service provider (B2B), helping to equip brick-and-mortar travel agencies with technology they could use to compete with the online-only players that were eating their lunch. We evolved from being one of those sellers of travel to an enabler.

The company started out largely penniless with no working capital. To get started, we borrowed money from a bank that was willing to lend to me $100, 000 in exchange for the personal guarantees of three known high-net individuals who were willing to sign, with me as the fourth guarantor. This gave me six months to hire a few people and to build our first Web site. In exchange for their guarantees, the guarantors received warrants to purchase stock in the company, which is how they achieved significant value in the end (roughly ten times their investment). I replaced that bank loan with another loan from Prodigy Services (the online service pioneer) which wanted to launch a vacation service for their membership. This essentially allowed me to replace bank debt with strategic partner debt: This was key in preserving equity. A year after we closed the Prodigy loan, we raised another $700,000 from a single investor who had a lot of entrepreneurial experience in the travel industry and had made a small fortune in the market in which we were operating. He understood what we were doing and brought strategic value because he had actual assets he wanted to deploy to help us grow our business.

That second debt financing became our last outside financing until we decided to shift our strategy and pursue a business-to-business play in which we hired a banker to help us raise money. That's when we started talking to venture capital, as well as strategic investors. We ended up getting a term sheet from a top-tier Northeast-based venture firm. We wanted to raise $16 million, which would enable us to buy three companies that were generating cash flow. So we were a dot-com business that was losing money, trying to buy profitable businesses that would become strategic assets through which we would distribute our technology to the brick-and-mortar travel industry. The companies we were purchasing were marketing firms that had been providing services to the retail travel world. We bought three of these companies, which gave us access to nearly 3,000 member travel agencies all across the country.

We were raising money to pursue these buy-outs and were able to generate interest also from a strategic investor, a global distribution system (GDS) whose primary business is in providing travel inventory to travel agents. The company was interested in making this investment, which was technically in the form of a loan with a warrant that enabled them to convert their loan into stock in the company at a predetermined share price. They did not negotiate the warrant term and were really interested in the strategic relationship we presented them. From our point of view, this was more compelling than the VC money that was very specific about the valuation we were to place on the business. The strategic investor invested $16 million, and we acquired the three businesses.

Soon thereafter we were approached by our chief competitor in this market, which was funded by a leading private equity firm. Our competitor was pursuing a similar strategy and had bought five companies, had deeper pockets than we did, and had approached us about merging our two companies to make this colossus in the travel marketing world with 9,000 travel agencies and 30 percent market share. We pursued and completed the merger and soon thereafter attempted to take advantage of the closing window to do an IPO. We never went to market and instead decided to pursue a buyer. The GDS that had originally provided $16 million in capital to my company ended up acquiring the entire company for slightly under $100 million in cash.

AW: How did your expectations of financing the business differ from what actually happened?

AM: When I founded Vacation.com, I had come off two start-ups, both of which ended for me without any significant wealth.

Both companies are now prospering, but none of the founders ever made any substantial money. I approached the launch and financing of Vacation.com with a bootstrap mentality. It definitely was during the middle of a rational economy and post-recession. The segment I was focusing on was leisure travel, which had been devastated by the Gulf War. So investors were leery of the space. My expectations were not lofty. I was willing to give up a significant portion of my company and my stock to get the company funded. The initial loan guarantors and warrant holders received approximately 7.5 percent of the stock in the company at that time in exchange for their guarantees and signatures. I thought this was a good deal at the time because it gave me six months to get the business up and running and generate nominal revenue.

As things became frothier with respect to valuations in the dot-com economy, we were able to raise capital without experiencing enormous dilution. My expectations were that we would have to raise money and negotiate hard on valuation, but it turned out that this was not the case. Some entrepreneurs in more rational economies may not have this expectation, but it is clearly a reality in the private equity and venture financing arena. Had the markets not worked as much in my favor, I believe I would probably have still have been able to build a healthy company, but I would not have been able to preserve as much equity.

AW: How much time did you spend working on the company's financing needs, and how did that differ from your expectations?

AM: As a founder and majority shareholder, I was always thinking about this and spent probably half of my time raising money. It seemed to have gone away only once we raised $16 million from the strategic GDS partner. So I spent a good five years focused on raising money and was constantly worried about making payroll. I did expect this was not going to be easy.

AW: In addition to strategic investment, what are some of the other examples of alternatives to venture financing that were helpful to you?

AM: As it turns out, the initial idea of getting a bank to lend me money and only asking for guarantees was a very smart idea. I always give this idea to someone who is looking to start a company. It is so much easier to get someone to sign a guarantee than to write a check, if you can find a bank that is willing to lend money on a decent business idea and take as collateral the signatures of some wealthy people the bank may not know directly but may know of by reputation or by virtue of their position in society. That enabled me to keep a significant portion of the company. Usually when people start things raw, they have to give up a significant piece of equity in the company. Ten years ago, $100,000 was more money than it is today, but it was enough to get us going because I was not taking salary and was working out of my house. We did also have success in pursuing a form of vendor financing. One travel company we were doing business with was willing to give us an advance on commissions we would later earn. This form of creditor financing really helped us manage our precious cash.

AW: If you or your group of founders personally lost majority control, at what stage did that happen, and how did you feel about it?

AM: It happened only when we merged with our competitor. Before the merger, I still held 60 percent of the equity in the company I had founded. I was able to maintain this even after the $16 million financing from the GDS strategic investor. This is really an indication of how much the market by 1999 played in favor of entrepreneurs. It might have been significantly less favorable in a more rational environment.

After the merger with our competitor, Travel Associates Network, which was venture-backed, I was still able to retain almost 20 percent of the common. I gave up majority control and did not feel terrible about that. The interests of the other members of the expanded and new team were very well aligned. Everyone was very motivated to monetize the investment; the CEO of the new group clearly was well positioned to be CEO. I became chairman, founder and chief information officer. We complemented each other well. He was older. I had the dot-com visionary label. We had a very good partnership, so I was willing to surrender operational control and give up equity control because we were all going to be singing from the same hymn book.

AW: Do you feel your business was valued fairly at each stage of financing?

AM: The one point at which we felt there was a disconnect between valuations was about the time the market came off in late 1999/2000, and we decided not to take the company public. We were interviewing investment banks. We were told by an unnamed investment bank that they could see the value of our business placed at upwards of $300 million. Subsequently, when we had offers in the region of $100 million to acquire the company, we felt ripped off, just because of the expectations that had been set previously. The reality sank in and, thankfully, more sober minds prevailed. The private equity firm that had backed the company with which the company I founded had merged was not willing to entertain the fantasy of hanging onto the company with the idea that we would be able to find a buyer or perhaps later go public at such a valuation. They were much more pragmatic in saying let's declare victory and live to fight another day.

AW: Discuss the value the venture capital component brought to Vacation.com.

AM: Our relationship with the private equity group that backed the company we merged with was very positive. Their role as experienced private equity investors who had been through both good times and bad carried the day. People who were younger and had entrepreneurial experience, like me, were being seduced by the dot-com frenzy, unable to see forest for the trees: We kept hearing about billion-dollar market caps! The presence of some "gray hair" and maturity that disciplined our collective expectations proved to be the best part of the whole mix because, had we been left to our own devices, chances are we would never have achieved the favorable outcome we did, in which everyone did reasonably well and made money.

AW: Elaborate on times when you felt your interests were out of alignment with those of your VC investors and how you resolved those situations.

AM: No one ever got diluted; no one ever took a hair cut; there were no cram-downs; and no one was ever really harmed economically. In the whole strategic decision-making process – how we ran the business, who we hired – sometimes there were disagreements, but these really did not come from our investors. They were management team issues. The exit decision was the only point of real contention. But in hindsight, had we negotiated harder or waited four to six months later, the acquiring entity might not have done the deal. Had we waited, or been greedy, we might not have been able to sell, particularly with the events of 9/11, when the travel industry imploded. The deal was closed in December 2000. On this, our interests never diverged; we were all marching to the same drummer.

AW: Did you ever consider using a placement agent? Talk about the advantages and disadvantages of doing so and your experiences.

AM: The placement agent we used is a small boutique investment bank in Connecticut called Interactive Capital Partners. I knew them through business school relationships. Their specialty was raising money for private companies at our stage. We hired them to make introductions to venture firms; many venture firms were very dismissive of the whole notion of enabling travel agents. The conventional wisdom at the time among many venture firms was that the travel agency world was going to disappear and that nothing could help it, which has turned out not to be the case. We needed to find an investor who was sympathetic to our argument and understood it as a result of experience. Interactive Capital was able to find us such an investor. One of the partners at the venture firm we were introduced to, and which eventually gave us a term sheet, came from a family who owned a travel agency and therefore understood our business hypothesis and had insight.

AW: What was your personal experience with venture investors, and how did their requirements conflict with your business objectives?

AM: One of the things that were most troubling was what is known as participating preferred. It is a somewhat euphemistic term for double-dipping: The investors get their money back and then participate on a pro-rata basis alongside the common. They get their proportional stake in the common, which means that if the company does not sell for much more than the venture investment, the common get very little. That particular term was very one-sided in our opinion, but I now know it is quite standard. In any event, I could not at the time persuade my other shareholders to accept this term. These shareholders were the principal shareholders of the companies we were acquiring for a combination of cash and stock. In a roll-up scenario, the venture capital-proposed participating preferred structure was a big turn-off to companies whose common stockholders saw that their value and shareholding position was potentially being placed as secondary to preferred stockholders. The participating preferred was a real deal-killer. The companies we were buying were largely owned by founders, and many of them were not sophisticated. They did not understand nuances and the plusses and minuses of that particular deal term, which really compensates for the risk any particular venture firm takes when anticipating execution of a strategy. My other shareholders saw that they had companies that were valuable, built over long careers, that were making money and paying them salaries and bonuses. They did not want to jeopardize their reward when they were selling their companies by taking paper with uncertain value. They were being asked to give up control to a new company and to management. There were also board control and anti-dilution provisions that were a bit unpleasant.

AW: What was your motivation in choosing a strategic investor, and how well were they aligned with the goals of your company?

AM: My other shareholders really liked the idea of a strategic investor who could bring more than just money to the equation. They saw that the GDS brought lots of tangible value. The dilemma with strategic money, though, is that it typically comes with more strings attached – exclusivities and rights to acquire the company at some future time, for example – but it also sometimes brings great value beyond money. That's what carried the day.

The reason the GDS was motivated to invest in us is that they saw their investment as a way to gain market share. By locking us up and making us sign an exclusive agreement in which they became the only GDS to be offered to our membership, we also gained some economic advantage. So that became both a benefit and a curse. Not all of our members wanted to be exclusive with the GDS; some had other preferences. On one hand, we got financing to do our deal and had a preferred strategic relationship that paid us money and offered our member agencies an incentive to make more money if they switched over to them. On the other hand, it was not universally applauded by our membership. So the strategic money (and elements of that partnership agreement that went with the financing) proved to be a double-edged sword – good in some ways and not good in others. Aside from that, it was a positive because ultimately they enabled us to exit our investment and have a successful outcome.

AW: What are some of the things entrepreneurs need to look out for in a term sheet?

AM: You need to consider what will happen if things do and don't go well. What can happen to you as a stakeholder? Can you be kicked out by the venture management if they do not like what you are doing? If so, what are the provisions for your separation? Think about that up-front. Not a lot of people think about that, and they end up outside the company they founded with very little safety net. That's one set of caveats.

Vesting is something to look at closely. Everyone should vest, including founders. Even if the founder never vested his own shares, professional investors will most likely insist that a portion of that will come under some sort of a stock restriction agreement. This is an important way of keeping the management team in place and, in the event of a departure of a founding team member, having equity available to provide to new management.

Liquidation preference is also clearly something people need to be aware of, but I don't think there is any possible way to avoid this when you are doing growth equity and getting start-up or early expansion-phase capital, which perceives risk. When you are doing later-stage mezzanine financing, then this is not as big an issue.

The market will pretty much dictate a lot of conditions. In our case, our placement agent was an important sounding board, and it was clear that the market was saying that if we wanted to take VC money, we needed to accept ceding control over certain important decisions at the board level.

AW: What is your biggest piece of advice to other entrepreneurs who are just beginning the financing process?

AM: Try to get as far as you can with friends and family, and use guaranteed bank financing, if possible. It may or may not be available under certain market conditions, but it is a great way to buy yourself six months to a year if you can bootstrap your business and get cash through the guarantees, instead of having to get people to write checks. A debt instrument really does help. The other thing – this sounds like a cliché – is to get to know who your investors are as people and make sure you really like them. Everything is always great during the romancing phase, when everyone loves each other and gets along. But check references of investors to make sure they are not crazy people who can turn into unpleasant partners. The human side is kind of a cliché, but I think it is really important.

Placement Agents – Terms of Engagement: Discussion with Ginny Davis Wilmerding

Andrew McKee's experience points to the range of financing sources that growing, early-stage companies can tap. Whereas it is natural to want to manage and control the financing process oneself, Vacation.com's experience pointed to the usefulness of engaging an outside party to source capital from venture investors. To drill down and explore the merits of using third parties to manage the capital raising process, the second section of this chapter focuses on the use of placement agents and the terms of engagement in working with such agents.

Venture firms can, of course, look upon deals that are packaged by placement agents with some degree of suspicion. Many firms have a predisposition to invest in deals that are introduced to them through pre-existing relationships. This is where the value of a placement agent is clearly put to the test. An agent's value is truly in his organization's ability to keep an active and interested list of investors engaged in looking at deals the placement agent represents.

The interview that follows represents a discussion with Ginny Davis Wilmerding, who was vice president, business development, for two Massachusetts-based technology start-ups, JuniorNet Corporation and Mutualfunds.com. Before working for these two technology start-ups, she was regional director for AT&T WorldNet Asia Pacific. She currently works in the Division of Research at Harvard Business School. Her experience in managing the private placement process at the two startups is the focus of the interview that follows. The first of the two technology companies for which she worked, JuniorNet, successfully completed a private placement of a little more than $70 million in 1999. The second, Mutualfunds.com, pursued a placement of $10 million, although it closed down before completing the fundraising process.

This discussion is particularly useful because it highlights the trade-offs in working with an outsourced entity in managing the fundraising process, the qualities you should look for in choosing a placement agent, and perhaps most importantly, the terms under which you can expect to work when engaging a placement agent.

Alex Wilmerding: What was your role in your company's financing process?

Ginny Davis Wilmerding: I was VP Business Development for both companies, and the reason I got very involved in the private placement process at the time was that these companies were too small to have a CFO, and I was handling all of the interaction with our attorneys regarding partnerships and corporate matters, in addition to helping the CEOs with corporate development and strategic planning. So I became the main person working with placement agents, in addition to the attorneys.

AW: Why did you choose to use placement agents in both instances?

GW: We needed to use placement agents to get our message out to a wider circle of investors. In a private company you cannot make any public solicitations for funds. So you need a network of people who are willing to put up large amounts of money, and the professional people who do that are private placement agents, such as investment banks, who typically have connections with investors and large institutions that might be interested. Plus, raising capital is a very time-consuming process, even with an agent, not to mention without one. So if you are a small company that is very lean, it is difficult to focus on running the company and raising money at the same time with no outside help.

AW: Can you talk about the types of firms you looked at and why you chose to work with the ones you chose?

GW: The time period in which we worked on these placements was a factor. The first company, JuniorNet, was raising money in the fall of 1998 and winter of 1999 – a very good time for small start-up companies to raise capital. All the big investment banks had an appetite to raise money for small start-ups. We actually got to choose between a few large Wall Street banks that were all trying to get our business, so we never considered dealing with smaller firms. When the size of the offering is large enough, in this case in excess of $20 million, fee is interesting enough to a large bank.

In the case of Mutualfunds.com, we worked with smaller boutique private placement agents. The amount of money we were hoping to raise in that instance was about $10 million. In the spring of 2000, start-ups could not expect to raise as much money as in the 1998-1999 period, so we worked exclusively with small firms. We explored working with a New York-based group named Fieldstone Services Corp. and a Boston-based company called Keen Partners, as well as with a small, two-person shop.

AW: How might an entrepreneur source and select a placement agent?

GW: Often existing lead investors in a company will have worked with placement agents before and can provide referrals. That is how we were introduced to Fieldstone. The other way is through venture capitalists or investors you may be trying to solicit for funds. That is how we heard about Keen and a couple of others.

AW: Talk about the process of working with a placement agent and the time involved.

GW: In every deal, a private placement memorandum (PPM) is produced on the company and becomes the sales document an agent uses to introduce the deal to potential investors. Typically, the bank cannot and isn't willing to complete it without extensive cooperation from the company; and more typically the company itself is responsible for writing this document and producing financial projections. The company will work jointly with the agent, but 70 percent to 80 percent of the work tends to be done by the company, and rightly so – it is the statement of your strategic and operating plans, and it describes your management, structure, company history, and projections. If your company has never done a concise, professional job of putting this in writing, it may take two to three months to write and finalize such a document and have it reviewed by attorneys.

The numbers used in the projections in the PPM are very important because they are used by investors as a basis for valuing the company. One thing to realize is that PPMs are usually widely distributed. What you might have previously considered confidential information will be widely distributed, potentially to hundreds of investors. In addition, there will be a road show, which will require that a presentation be prepared to go along with the PPM. The whole fund raising process can easily take six months, though there are a lot of variables.

AW: Did you find that the process was helpful?

GW: Yes, I did because it forces a company to make strategic decisions about its future directions and plans. It can be a very good catalyst to have an outsider scrutinizing your business and operating plans. On the downside, however, you can get a lot of pressure to make the numbers look better than you can realistically hope for and to make your marketing plan look as compelling as possible. Placement agents want the picture to look as positive as possible, so it is important to keep in mind that ultimately the management team of the company will have to defend the plan and operate to it.

AW: Speak about some of the qualities and value-add you looked for in the different types of placement organizations you explored working with.

GW: The reputation of the firm was very important to us. Also very important was the agent's experience in dealing with our type of company. In the case of Mutualfunds.com, we did not want someone who had experience raising money only in, say, the oil and gas industry and who had none in financial services. We also wanted someone familiar with our dot-com profile. In addition, we considered how good we felt an agent's connections might be to appropriate potential investors. If they particularly knew the industry we were in and had a large group of clients that appeared to be a good fit, that was compelling. One benefit of working with some of the larger Wall Street firms is that their placement arm may have a good relationship with the private client services group whose own clients may have an interest in a direct investment. Investment bank analyst coverage was a criterion we considered in the 1998-1999 time frame, but considering the changes that have most recently separated analyst and investment banking functions, this is now not so relevant. Then, it was important that you met the analyst; also the bank would not want to work with you unless the analyst liked your company.

AW: Talk about placement fee structures, commissions, and terms.

GW: Placement agents charge a very wide range of fees – between 5 percent and 10 percent and sometimes as high as 12 percent of what you raise. The fee as a percentage should be lower as the amount of capital you raise increases. Placement agents managing small capital raises will expect a higher fee because the work involved is almost the same as for a larger raise.

Almost always the fee is divided into two pieces – cash and equity. The cash fee is normally the largest and on the lower end could be 5 per cent of the cash raised. In the case of a $10 million raise, this would represent $200,000.

The equity fee might range between 3 percent and 5 percent and is on top of the cash compensation. Although this is an oversimplification, the equity is usually in one of two forms. It can be a percent of the total equity raised from investors in the form of shares awarded at closing, or it can be in the form of warrants. The placement agent would have the right to exercise these at some future point. The terms can get very tricky here, so it is critical to understand what is actually being asked for.

Agents, particularly smaller ones, will also likely ask for a retainer. For smaller ones, a retainer of $20,000 or more is not unusual because they have their own cash flow needs and are not likely to be handling a high number of clients.

AW: Can you talk about some of the deal terms that are most important when negotiating a placement agent agreement?

GW: The most important terms are in the general areas of compensation and control. In negotiating the agent's compensation, you may be able to get the fee as a percentage down. You may also be able to reduce fees on money raised from investors who are known to you or who you bring to the table without the placement agent's introduction or help. That is something to negotiate.

In terms of control, placement agents will look for a term of exclusivity, as well as for rights to work with you in the future. The agent typically requires the exclusive right to represent you in the fund raising process for a period of time. You can limit an engagement agreement to six months; some may be 12 months. In the heyday of the Internet boom, banks often wanted to lock you in, in case you did a future financing or an IPO. (The IPO piece is further off for most companies in today's environment.) My recommendation is to weaken these rights so that you are not absolutely required to use a firm you may or may not wish to work with in the future. Instead, they might get first consideration or something more vaguely worded. Normally, there is not room for a lot of negotiation in a number of other areas in these documents. You will need to keep in mind that you will have to reimburse a placement agent's travel and legal expenses and budget accordingly. This expense can be in the range of $75,000.

AW: Describe some of the intangibles you would look for in a placement agent.

GW: I think it is very important that you like and respect the people because you will spend a significant amount of time working with them. We turned down one of the agents we considered working with at one of the companies I worked for partly because of fee structure, but largely because we did not feel we had a good rapport with one of the top people involved.

APPENDIX

Appendix A

Sample Term Sheet

The sample term sheet provided below reflects the "neutral" form of language for each term as analyzed in Chapter Three of *Term Sheets and Valuations* and is included here as a reference. For a complete analysis and range of language incorporating the three perspectives, *Term Sheets and Valuations* may be a helpful reference. The chapter assumes that each term in a term sheet can be written to be "investor-favorable," "neutral," or "company-favorable" and provides analysis of the language of each term when written from these three perspectives.

[Company Name]
[Term Sheet Date]

MEMORANDUM OF TERMS FOR PRIVATE PLACEMENT OF EQUITY SECURITIES

[   ] Ventures, L.P., and [   ] (the "Investors") are prepared to invest $ [   ] million in [   ]   (the "Company") under the terms contained in this term sheet. With the exception of the section of this agreement relating to expenses, this term sheet is a non-binding document prepared for discussion purposes only, and the proposed investment is specifically subject to customary stock purchase agreements, legal due diligence, and other conditions precedent contained herein, all satisfactory to the Investors in their sole discretion.

[Other Company or deal-specific terms.]

New Securities Offered: Newly issued shares of the Company's Series [A] Preferred (the "Preferred")

Total Amount Raised: [$]

Number of Shares: [/ To be determined to result in the Post-financing Capitalization below.]

Purchase Price Per Share: [$ / To be determined to result in the Post-financing Capitalization below (the "Original Purchase Price").]

Post-Financing Capitalization:
Common Stock
Founders:

[Name]	[	]
[Name]	[	]
[Name]	[	]
Sub-Total	[	]

Stock Option Program

[CEO]	[	]
[Others]	[	]
Sub-Total	[	]

Preferred Stock

[__] Ventures, L.P.,	[	]
[Co-Investor(s)][	]	
Sub-Total	[	]
Total Common Equivalent	[	]

Total Enterprise Value [_____]

Dividend Provisions:

The holders of the Series [A] Preferred shall be entitled to receive non-cumulative dividends in preference to any dividend on the Common Stock at the rate of 8 percent of the Original Purchase Price per annum, when and as declared by the Board of Directors. The Series [A] Preferred also will participate pro rata in any dividends paid on the Common Stock on an as-converted basis.

Liquidation Preference:

In the event of any liquidation or winding up of the Company, the holders of the Series [A] Preferred shall be entitled to receive in preference to the holders of the Common Stock a per share amount equal to the Original Purchase Price plus any declared but unpaid dividends (the "Liquidation Preference"). After the payment of the Liquidation Preference to the holders of the Series [A] Preferred, the remaining assets shall be distributed ratably to the holders of the Common Stock and the Series [A] Preferred on a Common Stock equivalent basis; provided that the holders of Series [A] Preferred will stop participating once they have received a total liquidation amount equal to [three] times the Original Purchase Price. A merger, acquisition, sale of voting control, or sale of substantially all of the assets of the Company in which the shareholders of the Company do not own a majority of the outstanding shares of the surviving corporation shall be deemed to be a liquidation.

Redemption:

Redemption at Option of Investors:

At the election of the holders of at least [two thirds] of the Series [A] Preferred, the Company shall redeem the outstanding Series [A] Preferred in three equal annual installments beginning on the [fifth] anniversary of the Closing. Such redemptions shall be at a purchase price equal to the Original Purchase Price plus declared and unpaid dividends.

Conversion:

The holders of the Series [A] Preferred shall have the right to convert the Series [A] Preferred, at any time, into shares of Common Stock. The initial conversion rate shall be 1:1, subject to adjustment as provided below.

Automatic Conversion:

The Series [A] Preferred shall be automatically converted into Common Stock, at the then applicable conversion price, (i) in the event that the holders of at least two thirds of the outstanding Series [A] Preferred consent to such conversion or (ii) upon the closing of a firmly underwritten public offering of shares of Common Stock of the Company at a per share price not less than [2 times the Original Purchase Price] per share and for a total offering with gross proceeds to the Company of not less than $25 million (a "Qualified IPO").

Anti-dilution Provisions:

The conversion price of the Series [A] Preferred will be then subject to a weighted average adjustment (based on all outstanding shares of Preferred and Common Stock) to reduce dilution in the event that the Company issues additional equity securities (other than the reserved employee shares described under "Employee Pool") at a purchase price less than the applicable conversion price. The conversion price will also be subject to proportional adjustment for stock splits, stock dividends, recapitalizations, and the like. This anti-dilution protection is subject to a play-or-lose provision that provides that adjustments will be made to the Series [A] Conversion Price only if the Series [A] holder participates in such dilutive offering to the extent of its pro rata equity interest in the Preferred. Any investor who does not participate in a future financing forfeits the benefits of dilution protection [for all future rounds of financing/only for that financing round].

Voting Rights:

The Series [A] Preferred will vote together with the Common Stock and not as a separate class except as specifically provided herein or as otherwise required by law. Each share of Series [A] Preferred shall have a number of votes equal to the number of shares of Common Stock then issuable upon conversion of such share of Series [A] Preferred.

Protective Provisions:

For so long as at least [one-half of the shares originally issued] shares of Series [A] Preferred remain outstanding, consent of the holders of at least two thirds of the Series [A] Preferred shall be required for any action that (i) alters or changes the rights, preferences, or privileges of the Series [A] Preferred; (ii) increases or decreases the authorized number of shares of Common or Preferred Stock; (iii) creates (by reclassification or otherwise) any new class or series of shares having rights, preferences, or privileges senior to or pari passu with the Series [A] Preferred; (iv) results in the redemption of any shares of Common Stock (other than pursuant to equity incentive agreements with service providers giving the Company the right to repurchase shares upon the termination of services); (v) results in any merger, other corporate reorganization, sale of control, or any transaction in which all or substantially all of the assets of the Company are sold; or (vi) amends or waives any provision of the Company's Certificate of Incorporation or Bylaws relative to the Series [A] Preferred.

Board Composition and Meetings:

The size of the Company's Board of Directors shall be set at [five]. The Board shall initially comprise [   ], [   ], [   ], [   ], and [   ]. At each meeting for the election of directors, the holders of the Series [A] Preferred, voting as a separate class, shall be entitled to elect one member of the Company's Board of Directors, the holders of Common Stock, voting as a separate class, shall be entitled to elect two members, and the remaining directors will be mutually agreed upon by the Common and Preferred. It is anticipated that the Company's CEO will occupy one of the remaining seats. Board of Directors meetings will be held at least four times per year. Until the Company is profitable or the Board otherwise agrees, Board meetings will be targeted for every two months, or six times per year.

Special Board Approval Items:

Board approval will be required for:

1. Hiring of all officers of the Company.
2. Any employment agreements (approval by a majority of disinterested Directors, or a Compensation Committee when established).
3. Compensation programs including base salaries and bonus programs for all officers and key employees (approval by a majority of disinterested Directors or a Compensation Committee when established).
4. All stock option programs as well as issuance of all stock and stock options (approval by a majority of disinterested Directors or a Compensation Committee when established).
5. Annual budgets, business plans, and financial plans.
6. All real estate leases or purchases.
7. Execution of entrance obligations or commitments, including capital equipment leases or purchases, with total value greater than $[   ] and which are outside the most recent business plan or budget approved by the Board of Directors.

Information Rights:

So long as an Investor continues to hold shares of Series [A] Preferred or Common Stock issued upon conversion of the Series [A] Preferred, the Company shall deliver to the Investor audited annual financial statements audited by a Big Five accounting firm and unaudited quarterly financial statements. So long as an Investor holds not less than [one quarter of the Shares originally issued] shares of Series [A] Preferred (or [one quarter of the Shares originally issued] shares of the Common Stock issued upon conversion of the Series [A] Preferred, or a combination of both), the Company will furnish the Investor with monthly financial statements compared against plan and will provide a copy of the Company's annual operating plan within 30 days prior to the beginning of the fiscal year. Each Investor shall also be entitled to standard inspection and visitation rights. These provisions shall terminate upon a public offering of the Company's Common Stock.

Registration Rights:

Demand Rights: If Investors holding more than 50 percent of the outstanding shares of Series [A] Preferred, including Common Stock issued on conversion of Series [A] Preferred ("Registrable Securities"), request that the Company file a Registration Statement having an aggregate offering price to the public of not less than $5,000,000, the Company will use its best efforts to cause such shares to be registered; provided, however, that the Company shall not be obligated to effect any such registration prior to the third anniversary of the Closing. The Company shall have the right to delay such registration under certain circumstances for one period not in excess of ninety (90) days in any twelve (12) month period.

The Company shall not be obligated to effect more than two (2) registrations under these demand right provisions, and shall not be obligated to effect a registration (i) during the one hundred eighty (180) day period commencing with the date of the Company's initial public offering, or (ii) if it delivers notice to the holders of the Registrable Securities within thirty (30) days of any registration request of its intent to file a registration statement for such initial public offering within ninety (90) days.

Company Registration: The Investors shall be entitled to "piggy-back" registration rights on all registrations of the Company or on any demand registrations of any other investor subject to the right, however, of the Company and its underwriters to reduce the number of shares proposed to be registered pro rata in view of market conditions. If the Investors are so limited, however, no party shall sell shares in such registration other than the Company or the Investor, if any, invoking the demand registration. No shareholder of the Company shall be granted piggy-back registration rights that would reduce the number of shares includable by the holders of the Registrable Securities in such registration without the consent of the holders of at least two thirds of the Registrable Securities.

S-3 Rights: Investors shall be entitled to two (2) demand registrations on Form S-3 (if available to the Company) so long as such registered offerings are not less than $500,000.

Expenses: The Company shall bear registration expenses (exclusive of underwriting discounts and commissions) of all such demands, piggy-backs, and S-3 registrations (including the expense of one special counsel of the selling shareholders not to exceed $15,000).

Transfer of Rights: The registration rights may be transferred to (i) any partner or retired partner of any holder which is a partnership, (ii) any family member or trust for the benefit of any individual holder, or (iii) any transferee who acquires at least [one eighth of the shares originally issued] shares of Registrable Securities; provided the Company is given written notice thereof.

Lock-Up Provision: If requested by the Company and its underwriters, no Investor will sell its shares for a specified period (but not to exceed 180 days) following the effective date of the Company's initial public offering; provided that all officers, directors, and other 1 percent shareholders are similarly bound.

Other Provisions: Other provisions shall be contained in the Investor Rights Agreement with respect to registration rights as are reasonable, including cross-indemnification, the period of time in which the Registration Statement shall be kept effective, and underwriting arrangements.

Right of First Refusal:

Investors holding at least [one eighth of the shares originally issued] shares of Registrable Securities shall have the right in the event the Company proposes to offer equity securities to any person (other than securities issued pursuant to employee benefit plans or pursuant to acquisitions) to purchase their pro rata portion of such shares. Any securities not subscribed for by an eligible Investor may be reallocated among the other eligible Investors. Such right of first refusal will terminate upon a Qualified IPO.

Conditions Precedent:

This proposal is non-binding, and is specifically subject to:
(1) Completed due-diligence reviews satisfactory to [Investor] and Investors' counsel, specifically including review of [Investor Counsel].
(2) Customary stock purchase and related agreements satisfactory to [Investor] and Investors' counsel, including stock option plan.
(3) Both the Company and Investors will negotiate exclusively and in good faith toward an investment as outlined in this proposal and agree to "no-shop" provisions for reasonable and customary periods of time.

Purchase Agreement:

The investment shall be made pursuant to a Stock Purchase Agreement reasonably acceptable to the Company and the Investors, which agreement shall contain, among other things, appropriate representations and warranties of the Company, covenants of the Company reflecting the provisions set forth herein, and appropriate conditions of closing, including an opinion of counsel for the Company. The Stock Purchase Agreement shall provide that it may only be amended and any waivers thereunder shall only be made with the approval of the holders of two thirds of the Series [A] Preferred. Registration rights provisions may be amended or waived solely with the consent of the holders of two thirds of the Registrable Securities.

Employee Matters:

Employee Pool: Upon the Closing of this financing there will be [   ] shares of issued and outstanding Common Stock held by the Founders and an additional   [   ] shares of Common Stock reserved for future issuance to key employees. Promptly after the Closing, Messrs. [   ] and [   ] will be granted incentive stock options from the [   ] share pool in the amount of [   ] shares each exercisable at $0.10 per share, which options will vest in accordance with the following paragraph.

Stock Vesting: All stock and stock equivalents issued after the Closing to employees, directors, consultants and other service providers will be subject to vesting as follows: [20 percent to vest at the end of the first year following such issuance, with the remaining 80 percent to vest monthly over the next four years.] The repurchase option shall provide that upon termination of the employment of the shareholder, with or without cause, the Company or its assignee (to the extent permissible under applicable securities law qualification) retains the option to repurchase at cost any unvested shares held by such shareholder.

The outstanding Common Stock currently held by the Founders will be subject to similar vesting terms, provided that the Founders shall be credited with two years of vesting as of the Closing, with their remaining unvested shares to vest monthly over three years.

Restrictions on Sales: The Company shall have a right of first refusal on all transfers of Common Stock, subject to normal exceptions.

Proprietary Information and Inventions Agreement:

Each officer and employee of the Company shall enter into an acceptable proprietary information and inventions agreement.

Co-Sale Agreement: The shares of the Company's securities held by [   ], [   ], [   ] and [   ] (the "Founders") shall be made subject to a co-sale agreement (with certain reasonable exceptions) with the holders of the Series [A] Preferred such that the Founders may not sell, transfer or exchange their stock unless each holder of Series [A] Preferred has an opportunity to participate in the sale on a pro rata basis. This right of co-sale shall not apply to and shall terminate upon the Company's initial public offering.

Key-Man Insurance: The Company shall procure a key-man life insurance policy for [   ] in the amount of $1,000,000, naming the Company as beneficiary.

Closing Date:

[   ], 200[ ] (the "Closing Date").

Legal Counsel:

The Company shall select legal counsel acceptable to [Investor] ([   ]). Unless counsels agree otherwise, Investors' counsel [   ] shall draft the financing documents for review by Company counsel.

Expenses:

The Company shall pay the reasonable fees for one special counsel to the Investors, expected not to exceed $[25,000 – $35,000], and for Company counsel.

Finders:

The Company and the Investors shall each indemnify the other for any finder's fees for which either is responsible.

Appendix B

Administration and Compensation
of Boards and Advisory Boards

A Comprehensive Survey of Late-stage Venture-backed
Technology Companies, September 2002

Survey Overview
Introduction

BoardSeat conducted this survey because of considerable uncertainty on the part of many companies, investors, and professional advisors as to market rates for compensation of board directors and advisory board members of venture-backed companies. We also took the opportunity to ask some key questions about how venture-backed companies administer their boards and advisory boards.

These results represent the first comprehensive study of the administration and compensation of boards and advisory boards for private companies. We hope the survey will help answer some of the important questions surrounding these issues.

We welcome your comments, particularly on areas that should be addressed in future surveys. Please send your comments to: stephenfowler@boardseat.com.

Methodology

The activities of almost 100 companies are represented in our survey results. We sent a questionnaire concerning board director and advisory board practices and compensation to 400 private venture capital-backed companies, the majority of which had received more than $10 million in venture funding. Most companies had received backing by tier one venture capital firms. We received a response rate of approximately 25 percent, and, after excluding a number of surveys because of incomplete information, summarized the results from 91 completed surveys. Where information was incomplete or ambiguous, telephone interviews were used to clarify responses.

Size of Board of Directors

As companies raise more money, the board of directors tends to get bigger. The average board size for companies that had raised less than $10 million is 5.3 members; whereas, the average board size for companies that had raised more than $50 million is 6.7 members.

Average Number of Board Directors

Amount Raised ($ million)	Mean number of board directors
0-10	5.3
10-25	5.2
25-50	6.5
50+	6.7

Board Director Compensation

We calculated the equivalent number of shares a director would receive per annum to compare companies that had different vesting schedules. For example, a director receiving an initial stock grant of 40,000 shares vesting over 4 years is assumed to have an annual compensation of 10,000 shares. Using this figure and the number of fully diluted shares outstanding after the last financing round, we then calculated the percentage of fully diluted shares paid per annum.

For companies that raised under $10 million, the mean percentage of shares granted to independent board directors per annum is about 0.07-0.08 percent of the fully diluted shares. However, that number drops to less than 0.05 percent for companies that raised over $50 million.

Size of Advisory Board

More than half the companies we surveyed had some type of advisory board. Companies are more likely to have an advisory board in the early stages of development than in the more mature stages. Of the companies that had raised $10 million or less, 68.8 percent have an advisory board, as compared with only 37.5 percent of companies that had raised $50 million or more. There is a wide range in the number of advisors retained by companies, with the average advisory board size being about five members.

Average Number of Advisory Board Members

Amount Raised ($ million)	Percentage of Companies with Advisory Board	Mean Number of Advisors for Companies with Advisory Boards
0-10	68.8	4.8

10-25	63.2	4.7
25-50	53.1	5.6
50+	37.5	5.0

Advisory Board Compensation

As companies mature and become larger, they tend to pay a smaller percentage of equity to their advisory board members. Companies that had raised less than $10 million pay their advisors, on average, 0.043 percent per annum, which translates to about half that paid to board directors. Companies that had raised more than $50 million pay their advisors, on average, 0.013 percent per annum – about one quarter that paid to board directors.

Reprinted with Permission of BoardSeat
Copyright: BoardSeat.
All rights reserved.

Appendix C

Documents Likely to Be Requested During Due Diligence

Corporate Records
1. Articles of Incorporation and By-Laws
2. Board of directors and board of directors committee meetings' minutes
3. Form of stock certificates and records of stock issuances
4. Minutes of stockholders meetings
5. Annual/quarterly reports and other communications to stockholders since inception
6. Press clippings and releases since inception

Governmental Regulations and Filings
1. Any filings or material correspondence with state or federal regulatory agencies
2. If applicable, any material governmental permits, licenses

Financings
1. All documents and agreements recording debt
2. Correspondence with lenders and any documents and agreements regarding other financing facilities
3. Offering documents produced for any proposed or completed financing since founding

Operating Agreements
1. Sales, agency, distribution, and advertising contracts
2. Joint venture, partnership, and alliance agreements
3. Warranties of the company
4. Licensing agreements, franchises, and conditional sales contracts

5. Supply or requirement contracts (including licenses involving technology transfer)
6. Employment agreements, compensation and benefit program documentation, consulting agreements, and agreements with management
7. Leases

Inter-company Agreements and Agreements with Affiliates

1. Inter-company agreements and services provisions

Other Agreements

1. Insurance policies
2. Patents and patent applications, trademarks, brands, and copyrights
3. Documents relating to major acquisitions or dispositions

Additionally...

1. A summary of and documentation related to significant litigation, administrative proceedings, and governmental investigations, either pending or closed
2. Any other agreements to which the company is a party, or is bound, including non-compete agreements or agreements that may require or prohibit future activities
3. Directors' and officers' questionnaires prepared in connection with current offering
4. Any other documents or information that are significant or should be considered and reviewed in making disclosures regarding the business and financial condition of the company to prospective investors

Appendix D

Time Value of Money Tables

The following two tables are useful in calculating the time value of money and in assessing venture investors' expectations.

Present Value

Years/Rate	5%	10%	15%	20%	25%	30%	40%
3	.86	.75	.66	.58	.51	.46	.36
5	.78	.62	.50	.40	.33	.27	.19
10	.61	.39	.25	.16	.11	.07	.03
15	.48	.24	.12	.06	.04	.02	.01
20	.38	.15	.06	.03	.01	.01	-
25	.30	.09	.03	.01	-	-	-

IRR

Multiple/Years	2X %	2.5X	3X	3.5X	4X	5X	6X	8X	10X
2	41	58	73	87	100	124	145	183	216
3	26	36	44	52	59	71	82	100	115
4	19	26	32	37	41	49	56	68	78
5	15	20	25	28	32	38	43	52	58
6	12	16	20	23	26	31	35	41	47
7	10	14	17	20	22	26	29	35	39
8	9	12	15	17	19	22	25	30	33
9	8	11	13	15	17	20	22	26	29
10	7	10	12	13	15	17	20	23	26

Information provided by Coller Capital

ABOUT THE AUTHOR

Alex Wilmerding is a principal at Boston Capital Ventures, a venture firm specializing primarily in private equity direct investments in companies with an information technology (IT) software and services focus. Wilmerding has over ten years of private equity and general management operating experience in the IT software, Internet, transportation, and hospitality industries.

At BCV, Wilmerding serves as a director on the boards of portfolio companies, including HUBX, Inc., a Waltham, Massachusetts-based revenue management and distribution services solutions provider to the hospitality industry; FareChase, Inc., a New York, New York-based travel software provider; and KhiMetrics, Inc., the Scottsdale, Arizona-based developer of the first revenue management system designed to help retailers maximize revenue and profits. Wilmerding also serves as an observer to the board of Exa Corporation, the Bedford, Massachusetts-based developer of fluid flow simulation software for wind tunnel applications, as well as advisor to high-growth private companies.

In the not-for-profit arena, Wilmerding serves as an officer and trustee of the Yale-China Association, an organization based in New Haven, Connecticut, which facilitates educational, environmental, legal, and medical exchanges between the United States and China. A great believer in the value of international work experience, he is fluent in Mandarin and has held management positions in the Peoples Republic of China, as well as in Hong Kong, Taiwan, and Indonesia.

Wilmerding earned his BA in history from Yale University and his MBA in finance and organizational management from the Columbia Business School. He lives in the Boston area with his wife Ginny and son Nicholas. Questions or comments regarding this book can be addressed to wilmerding@hotmail.com.